Anti-Inflammatory Diet Cookbook for Beginners:

1500 Days of Quick & Easy Recipes That Are Worth Trying, Including 30-Day Meal Plan. Decrease the Body Inflammation, Balancing Hormones and Boost Your Immune System.

Lisa Mckeith

Table of Content

Introduction

Anti-inflammatory foods are foods that have been shown to have anti-inflammatory properties and can help reduce inflammation in the body. Inflammation is a natural response of the body to injury or infection, but chronic inflammation has been linked to the development of various chronic diseases such as heart disease, diabetes, cancer, and autoimmune disorders.

Here are some benefits of taking anti-inflammatory recipes:

- **Improved cardiovascular health:** Many anti-inflammatory foods, such as fatty fish and nuts, are high in omega-3 fatty acids, which have been shown to have a beneficial effect on heart health by reducing inflammation and preventing the formation of blood clots.

- **Improved joint health:** Anti-inflammatory foods can help reduce inflammation and pain in the joints, making them a great option for people with conditions such as rheumatoid arthritis.

- **Improved brain function:** Omega-3 fatty acids found in fish and nuts have been shown to improve brain function and may reduce the risk of cognitive decline and dementia.

- **Weight management:** Anti-inflammatory foods are often nutrient-dense and low in calories, making them a great option for weight management.

- **Stronger immunity:** Many anti-inflammatory foods, such as fruits and vegetables, are high in antioxidants and other nutrients that can help boost the immune system.

- **Better digestion:** Some anti-inflammatory foods, such as ginger and turmeric, have been shown to have a beneficial effect on digestion and may help reduce bloating and gas.

- **Improved skin health:** Some anti-inflammatory foods, such as nuts, seeds, and fatty fish, are high in healthy fats and antioxidants that can help improve the appearance of the skin and reduce the risk of skin conditions such as acne. Therefore, to help the reader to benefit from the numerous advantages of anti-inflammatory foods, this cookbook contains about 120 classic inflammatory food recipes. Enjoy!

What Is

Chronic Inflammation?

Asymptomatic or low-grade chronic inflammation is the basis of chronic degenerative diseases and tumors. These diseases can be prevented or counteracted by adopting a healthy lifestyle and diet, even if eating habits are altered at a later age. A sedentary lifestyle, excess calories from food, an incorrect diet, and poor-quality food contribute to chronic inflammation. The accumulation of fat, particularly visceral obesity, determines the production of pro-inflammatory cytokines, which promote the formation of an inflammatory environment and the production of hormones (conversion of androgens into estradiol in adipose tissue), which predispose to tumors (endometrium, breast, colon). Furthermore, diets rich in industrial food and "junk food" alter the intestinal bacterial flora, causing dysbiosis, which increases and maintains the inflammatory state. To reduce this condition, it is necessary to decrease the inflammatory stimuli by leading an active life, carefully choosing the foods to be consumed at the various meals, their quantity, quality, and variety, concentrating the meals in a reduced number of hours or fasting and following a chronobiological consumption to maintain ideal body weight or lose weight.

If we take into consideration the macronutrients that are part of the daily diet, they can be broken down in percentage terms as follows: Carbohydrates = 55%, Lipids = 35%, and Proteins = 15%. Complex carbohydrates should be preferred

The anti-inflammatory food pyramid has at its base vegetables to be eaten every day and at the top red meat, processed and preserved meat, and sweets to be eaten only occasionally. Furthermore, a daily energy surplus should be avoided. In particular, the evening meal must be light and reduced in terms of carbohydrates and lipids.

Pro-inflammatory foods: these are foods that increase the levels of inflammatory cytokines and are therefore able to determine epigenetic modifications. These are foods with a high caloric density, with a high glycemic and insulinemic index, and rich in saturated fats, arachidonic acid (from which the body synthesizes pro-inflammatory prostaglandins), and hydrogenated polyunsaturated fatty acids.

Symptoms and Causes

of Inflammation

As regards the chronic inflammatory state, the classic laboratory markers could remain silent or normal, although the tissue damage continues silently.

Symptoms and signs can also be heterogeneous and frequently include:

- Generalized malaise
- Unexplained mood changes (e.g., swings of sadness)
- Persistent fatigue
- Lack of appetite
- Low libido
- Sleep disorders
- Less desire for stimuli and to be with others
- Increased blood pressure
- Alteration of blood fats

Chronic inflammation differs from acute inflammation in that it is persistent, of low intensity, and causes collateral damage to the tissues without resolving itself in a short time. The main causes of chronic inflammatory states are multiple and multifactorial, i.e., they derive from the intersection of genetic, environmental, biological, and lifestyle factors. The main ones are as follows:

- Chronic and relapsing infections
- Obesity
- Prolonged sedentary lifestyle
- Intestinal dysbiosis
- Unbalanced power supply
- Discomfort and psychological suffering
- Sleep disorders

How Important Is Lifestyle
In Chronic Inflammation?

Lifestyle can significantly affect chronic inflammatory diseases and how these diseases affect the body. Here are some of the most common recommendations for a healthy lifestyle for chronic inflammatory diseases:

- **Healthy Eating:** A diet of anti-inflammatory foods, such as fruits, vegetables, fish, and nuts, can help manage inflammation. Avoiding pro-inflammatory foods, such as sugar, saturated fats, and processed foods, can also be helpful.

- **Exercise:** Regular exercise can help reduce inflammation and improve overall health. It is recommended that you exercise moderately for at least 30 minutes a day.

- **Reduce stress:** Stress can make inflammation worse, so it's important to find effective ways to manage it, such as meditation, yoga, or therapy.

- **Sleep well:** Adequate sleep is important for overall health and can help manage inflammation. It is recommended to get at least 7-8 hours of sleep a night.

- **Avoid smoking and alcohol:** Smoking and alcohol abuse can worsen inflammation and compromise overall health.

It is important to note that lifestyle recommendations may vary based on the specific disease and individual situation. It is always best to discuss your options with your doctor before making any significant lifestyle changes.

Pro-Inflammatory
Foods to Avoid

They are foods that increase the levels of inflammatory cytokines and are, therefore, capable of causing epigenetic modifications. These are foods with a high caloric density, with a high glycemic and insulinemic index, and rich in saturated fats, arachidonic acid (from which the body synthesizes pro-inflammatory prostaglandins), and hydrogenated polyunsaturated fatty acids. Take note of the following foods so that you can avoid them:

- Foods with a high caloric density (rich in fat), with a high glycemic and insulinemic index.
- Red meats, but also white meats if coming from intensive farms, processed/processed meats (cured meats, sausages, hot dogs, frankfurters).
- Foods cooked at high temperatures (fried, grilled, grilled), which cause the formation of lipo peroxides.
- Cow's milk and dairy products from animals reared in intensive farms, aged cheeses rich in saturated fats.
- Butter and vegetable oils with a high content of omega-6 fatty acids (corn oil, sunflower oil, other vegetable oils), cooked oils (e.g., fried and sautéed), and margarine.
- Foods rich in hydrogenated polyunsaturated fatty acids: bakery products (industrial bread, sandwich bread, crackers, biscuits) and commercial pastry.
- Pre-cooked or industrially processed foods with additives and preservatives
- Excess salt
- Alcohol/spirits
- Sugar
- Sweets and industrial sweets
- Sodas and carbonated and sugary drinks, "zero" drinks, industrial fruit juices,

drinks sweetened with artificial sweeteners; foods polluted with pesticides and heavy metals

Anti-Inflammatory

Foods and Benefits

The anti-inflammatory diet, if followed correctly, is a model capable of preventing and/or counteracting the chronic inflammatory state of the body. The risk linked to a disordered lifestyle and diet can be modified by observing the timing of meals (the consumption of food in a limited time improves metabolic inflammation), by consuming foods with a lower glycemic and insulin index, improving the relationship between omega-6 and omega-3 fatty acids, avoiding foods that contain hydrogenated fatty acids, and engaging in daily moderate-intensity physical activity. You may consider including the following anti-inflammatory foods in your diet:

- Occasional and moderate consumption or elimination from the food pattern of foods and drinks that promote inflammation, particularly industrial foods.
- Regular consumption of foods rich in polyphenols with anti-inflammatory and antioxidant activity.
- Daily consumption of whole grains, including grains and ancient varieties of wheat.
- Daily and varied consumption of fresh seasonal vegetables, with a short supply chain, raw or steamed, in order to acquire the necessary nutrients to a greater extent.
- Regular consumption of legumes during the week (at least three portions).
- Moderate daily consumption of fresh seasonal fruit of different colors (5-color rule).
- Consumption of oily fish rich in omega-3 fatty acids; consumption of nuts and oilseeds.
- Use of extra virgin olive oil (evo), aromatic herbs, and spices to vary the taste of foods and macronutrients (carbohydrates, lipids, vegetable, and animal proteins)

during the food day and during the week, adapting them to work needs and motor activity;

- Reduce total daily calorie intake (moderately low-calorie diet).

Figura 1 - Table of Aliments

Food Pyramid With Anti-Inflammatory Characteristics

An anti-inflammatory food program must take into account the type of foods, their nutritional properties, and frequency of consumption. It can be structured in the shape of a pyramid, taking into consideration the daily consumption of healthy foods. At the base of the pyramid are organic or alternatively frozen vegetables to be consumed every day (3-4 portions), and at the top are red meat, processed and preserved meat, desserts, and sweets to be eaten only occasionally. Preference should be given to complex carbohydrates, unsaturated fatty acids (extra virgin olive oil, to be consumed in moderate quantities), omega-3 polyunsaturated fatty acids, and proteins of vegetable origin.

Figura 1 - Food-pyramid

BREAKFASTS

1. OVERNIGHT OATS WITH CHIA SEEDS, BERRIES, AND ALMOND MILK

This overnight oat recipe is a delicious and anti-inflammatory breakfast option, made with chia seeds, berries, and almond milk.
Prep time: 5 minutes | Cook time: None (overnight soak) | Serving: 1 | Yield: 1 serving

Ingredients
- 1/2 cup rolled oats
- 1/4 cup chia seeds
- 1/2 cup mixed berries
- 1/2 cup unsweetened almond milk
- 1 tablespoon honey (optional)

Method of preparation
1. In a mason jar or airtight container, combine the rolled oats, chia seeds, mixed berries, and almond milk.
2. Stir to combine, then add the honey (if using) and stir again.
3. Cover and refrigerate overnight.
4. In the morning, give the oats a good stir, then enjoy!

Nutritional fact: Serving size : 1 | Calories: 348 |Fat: 15g | Saturated Fat: 1g | Cholesterol: 0mg | Sodium: 70mg | Carbohydrates: 44g | Fiber: 12g | Sugar: 12g | Protein: 12g

2. GREEN SMOOTHIE WITH SPINACH, KALE, AVOCADO, AND GINGER

This green smoothie is packed with anti-inflammatory ingredients like spinach, kale, avocado, and ginger.
Prep time: 5 minutes | Cook time: None | Serving: 1 | Yield: 1 serving

Ingredients

- 1 cup baby spinach
- 1 cup kale
- 1/2 avocado
- 1/2 banana
- 1 inch piece of ginger
- 1 cup unsweetened almond milk

Method of preparation

1. In a blender, combine the spinach, kale, avocado, banana, ginger, and almond milk.
2. Blend until smooth and creamy.
3. Serve immediately and enjoy!

Nutritional fact: Serving size : 1 | Calories: 256 | Fat: 15g | Saturated Fat: 2g | Cholesterol: 0mg | Sodium: 111mg | Carbohydrates: 27g | Fiber: 9g | Sugar: 7g | Protein: 6g

3. TURMERIC LATTE WITH ALMOND MILK AND HONEY

This turmeric latte is a comforting and anti-inflammatory drink made with almond milk and honey.

Prep time: 5 minutes | Cook time: 5 minutes | Serving: 1 | Yield: 1 serving

Ingredients

- 1 cup unsweetened almond milk
- 1 teaspoon turmeric powder
- 1/4 teaspoon ground cinnamon
- 1/4 teaspoon ground ginger
- 1 tablespoon honey

Method of preparation

1. In a small saucepan, heat the almond milk over medium heat.
2. Add the turmeric, cinnamon, and ginger, and stir to combine.
3. Bring the mixture to a simmer, then remove from heat.

4. Stir in the honey, then pour into a mug and enjoy!

Nutritional fact: Serving size : 1 | Calories: 103 | Fat: 7g | Saturated Fat: 0g | Cholesterol: 0mg | Sodium: 132mg | Carbohydrates: 11g | Fiber: 1g | Sugar: 8g

4. QUINOA BOWL WITH VEGGIES, AVOCADO, AND A POACHED EGG

This quinoa bowl is a healthy and anti-inflammatory breakfast option, made with quinoa, veggies, avocado, and a poached egg.

Prep time: 10 minutes | Cook time: 15 minutes | Serving: 1 | Yield: 1 serving

Ingredients

- 1/2 cup quinoa, cooked
- 1/2 cup diced vegetables of your choice (such as bell peppers, mushrooms, and onions)
- 1/2 avocado, diced
- 1 egg
- Salt and pepper, to taste

Method of preparation

1. In a pan, sauté the vegetables with salt and pepper until cooked.
2. On a plate, add cooked quinoa and sautéed vegetables.
3. In a separate pan, poach the egg by cracking it into a simmering water, cook for 2-3 minutes.
4. Add diced avocado and poached egg on top of quinoa mixture.
5. Serve hot and enjoy!

Nutritional fact: Serving size : 1 | Calories: 449 | Fat: 24g | Saturated Fat: 3g | Cholesterol: 186mg | Sodium: 31mg |

Carbohydrates: 44g | Fiber: 12g | Sugar: 2g | Protein: 15g

5. SWEET POTATO TOAST WITH ALMOND BUTTER, BANANA, AND CINNAMON

This sweet potato toast is a delicious and anti-inflammatory breakfast option, made with sweet potato, almond butter, banana, and cinnamon.

Prep time: 5 minutes | Cook time: 10 minutes | Serving: 1 | Yield: 1 serving

Ingredients

- 1 sweet potato, sliced into 1/4 inch slices
- 1 tablespoon almond butter
- 1/2 banana, sliced
- 1/4 teaspoon ground cinnamon

METHOD OF PREPARATION

1. Preheat oven to 375°F (190°C).
2. Place sweet potato slices on a baking sheet and bake for 10-12 minutes, or until tender.
3. Remove from oven and spread almond butter on top of each slice.
4. Add banana slices and sprinkle with cinnamon.
5. Serve and enjoy!

Nutritional fact: Serving size : 1 | Calories: 285 | Fat: 12g | Saturated Fat: 1g | Cholesterol: 0mg | Sodium: 42mg | Carbohydrates: 42g | Fiber: 5g| Sugar: 13g | Protein: 5g

6. CHIA SEED PUDDING WITH BERRIES AND COCONUT MILK

This chia seed pudding is a healthy and anti-inflammatory breakfast option, made with chia seeds, berries, and coconut milk.

Prep time: 5 minutes | Cook time: None (overnight soak) | Serving: 1 | Yield: 1 serving

Ingredients

- 1/4 cup chia seeds
- 1 cup coconut milk
- 1/2 cup mixed berries
- 1 tablespoon honey (optional)

Method of preparation

1. In a mason jar or airtight container, combine the chia seeds, coconut milk, mixed berries, and honey (if using).
2. Stir to combine, then cover and refrigerate overnight.
3. In the morning, give the pudding a good stir, then enjoy!

Nutritional fact: Serving size : 1 | Calories: 407 | Fat: 36g | Saturated Fat: 29g | Cholesterol: 0mg | Sodium: 74mg | Carbohydrates: 25g | Fiber: 19g | Sugar: 6g | Protein: 7g

7. WHOLE GRAIN PANCAKES WITH BLUEBERRIES AND FLAXSEED

These pancakes are made with whole grains, blueberries, and flaxseed, making them a healthy and anti-inflammatory breakfast option.

Prep time: 10 minutes | Cook time: 20 minutes | Serving: 2 | Yield: 2 servings

Ingredients

- 1 cup whole wheat flour
- 1 teaspoon baking powder
- 1/2 teaspoon baking soda
- 1 tablespoon flaxseed
- 1/2 cup blueberries
- 1 egg
- 1 cup unsweetened almond milk
- 1 tablespoon honey (optional)

Method of preparation

1. In a mixing bowl, combine the flour, baking powder, baking soda, and flaxseed.
2. In a separate bowl, whisk the egg, then add in the almond milk and honey (if using).
3. Slowly pour the wet ingredients into the dry ingredients and stir until just combined.
4. Gently fold in blueberries.
5. Heat a non-stick pan over medium heat and spoon the batter into the pan, using about 1/4 cup per pancake.
6. Cook for about 2-3 minutes on each side, or until golden brown.
7. Serve warm with your favorite toppings.

Nutritional fact: Serving size : 2 | Calories: 243 | Fat: 6g | Saturated Fat: 1g | Cholesterol: 62mg | Sodium: 252mg | Carbohydrates: 41g | Fiber: 5g | Sugar: 12g | Protein: 9g

8. EGG SCRAMBLE WITH BELL PEPPERS, TOMATOES, AND SPINACH

This egg scramble is a healthy and anti-inflammatory breakfast option, made with eggs, bell peppers, tomatoes, and spinach.

Prep time: 5 minutes | Cook time: 10 minutes | Serving: 1 | Yield: 1 serving

Ingredients

- 2 eggs
- 1/4 cup diced bell peppers
- 1/4 cup diced tomatoes
- 1/4 cup spinach
- Salt and pepper, to taste
- 1 tablespoon olive oil

Method of preparation

1. Heat olive oil in a pan over medium heat.
2. Add bell peppers and tomatoes and sauté until they start to soften
3. Add the spinach and cook until wilted.
4. In a separate bowl, whisk the eggs with a pinch of salt and pepper.
5. Pour the eggs into the pan with the vegetables.
6. Cook, stirring occasionally, until the eggs are set.
7. Serve hot and enjoy!

Nutritional fact: Serving size : 1 | Calories: 174 | Fat: 13g | Saturated Fat: 3g | Cholesterol: 373mg | Sodium: 115mg | Carbohydrates: 5g | Fiber: 1g | Sugar: 2g | Protein: 12g

9. OMELET WITH MUSHROOMS, ONIONS, AND FETA CHEESE

This omelet is a healthy and anti-inflammatory breakfast option, made with eggs, mushrooms, onions, and feta cheese.

Prep time: 5 minutes | Cook time: 10 minutes | Serving: 1 | Yield: 1 serving

Ingredients

- 2 eggs
- 1/4 cup diced mushrooms
- 1/4 cup diced onions

- 2 tablespoons crumbled
- feta cheese
- Salt and pepper, to taste
- 1 tablespoon olive oil

Method of preparation

1. Heat olive oil in a pan over medium heat.
2. Add mushrooms and onions and sauté until they start to soften
3. In a separate bowl, whisk the eggs with a pinch of salt and pepper.
4. Pour the eggs into the pan with the vegetables.
5. Sprinkle feta cheese on top of the omelette.
6. Cook, until the eggs are set and cheese is melted.
7. Fold the omelette in half, and serve hot.

Nutritional fact: Serving size : 1 | Calories: 270 | Fat: 21g | Saturated Fat: 8g | Cholesterol: 372mg | Sodium: 456mg | Carbohydrates: 4g | Fiber: 1g | Sugar: 2g | Protein: 17g.

10. YOGURT BOWL WITH BERRIES, NUTS, AND SEEDS

This yogurt bowl is a healthy and anti-inflammatory breakfast option, made with yogurt, mixed berries, mixed nuts, and seeds.
Prep time: 5 minutes | Cook time: None | Serving: 1 | Yield: 1 serving

Ingredients
- 1 cup plain Greek yogurt
- 1/2 cup mixed berries
- 2 tablespoons mixed nuts and seeds (such as almonds, pumpkin seeds, and sunflower seeds)
- 1 tablespoon honey (optional)

Method of preparation

1. In a bowl, mix the yogurt and honey (if using) together.
2. Add the mixed berries, nuts, and seeds on top of the yogurt.
3. Serve immediately and enjoy!

Nutritional fact

Serving size : 1 | Calories: 348 | Fat: 20g | Saturated Fat: 3g | Cholesterol: 12mg | Sodium: 100mg | Carbohydrates: 25g | Fiber: 4g | Sugar: 18g | Protein: 20g

11. SMOOTHIE BOWL WITH SPINACH, BANANA, AND CHIA SEEDS

This smoothie bowl is a healthy and anti-inflammatory breakfast option, made with spinach, banana, and chia seeds.
Prep time: 5 minutes | Cook time: None | Serving: 1 | Yield: 1 serving

Ingredients
- 1 cup fresh spinach
- 1 banana
- 1 tablespoon chia seeds
- 1/2 cup unsweetened almond milk
- 1 tablespoon honey (optional)

Method of preparation

1. In a blender, combine the spinach, banana, chia seeds, almond milk, and honey (if using).
2. Blend until smooth and creamy.
3. Pour the mixture into a bowl and garnish with additional chia seeds, if desired.
4. Serve immediately and enjoy!

Nutritional fact: Serving size : 1 | Calories: 225 | Fat: 7g | Saturated Fat: 1g | Cholesterol: 0mg | Sodium: 68mg | Carbohydrates: 39g | Fiber: 9g | Sugar: 15g | Protein: 5g

12. BREAKFAST BURRITO WITH SWEET POTATOES, BLACK BEANS, AND AVOCADO

This breakfast burrito is a healthy and anti-inflammatory option, made with sweet potatoes, black beans, and avocado.
Prep time: 10 minutes | Cook time: 15 minutes | Serving: 1 | Yield: 1 serving

Ingredients
- 1 small sweet potato, diced
- 1/4 cup black beans, rinsed and drained
- 1/2 avocado, diced
- 1 flour tortilla
- Salt and pepper, to taste
- 1 tablespoon olive oil

Method of preparation
1. Heat olive oil in a pan over medium heat.
2. Add sweet potatoes and cook until tender.
3. Season with salt and pepper.
4. Add black beans to the pan and cook for an additional 2-3 minutes.
5. Heat the flour tortilla in a separate pan or microwave for a few seconds to make it more pliable.
6. On the tortilla, add the sweet potato and black bean mixture, diced avocado and roll up the tortilla.
7. Serve warm and enjoy!

Nutritional Fact: Serving size : 1 | Calories: 365 | Fat: 17g | Saturated Fat: 2g | Cholesterol: 0mg | Sodium: 216mg | Carbohydrates: 45g | Fiber: 12g | Sugar: 5g | Protein: 10g

13. BREAKFAST SALAD WITH MIXED GREENS, NUTS, AND BOILED EGG

This breakfast salad is a healthy and anti-inflammatory option, made with mixed greens, nuts, and boiled egg.
Prep time: 5 minutes | Cook time: 5 minutes | Serving: 1 | Yield: 1 serving

Ingredients
- 2 cups mixed greens
- 1/4 cup mixed nuts (such as almonds, pecans, and walnuts)
- 1 boiled egg, sliced
- 1 tablespoon olive oil
- 1 tablespoon lemon juice
- Salt and pepper, to taste

Method of preparation
1. In a bowl, mix the mixed greens, mixed nuts, and boiled egg.
2. In a small bowl, whisk together the olive oil, lemon juice, salt and pepper to make a simple dressing.
3. Pour the dressing over the salad and toss to combine.
4. Serve immediately and enjoy!

Nutritional fact
Serving size : 1 | Calories: 365 | Fat: 29g | Saturated Fat: 6g | Cholesterol: 186mg | Sodium: 118mg | Carbohydrates: 12g | Fiber: 4g | Sugar: 2g | Protein: 13g

14. AVOCADO TOAST WITH POACHED EGG AND SMOKED SALMON

This avocado toast is a healthy and anti-inflammatory option, made with avocado, poached egg, and smoked salmon.

Prep time: 5 minutes | Cook time: 5 minutes | Serving: 1 | Yield: 1 serving

Ingredients:

- 1 piece of whole grain bread
- 1/2 avocado, mashed
- 1 poached egg
- 2 oz smoked salmon
- Salt and pepper, to taste

METHOD OF PREPARATION:

1. Toast the bread until golden brown.
2. Spread mashed avocado on top of the toast.
3. Top the avocado toast with poached egg and smoked salmon.
4. Season with salt and pepper.
5. Serve warm and enjoy!

Nutritional fact: Serving size : 1 | Calories: 348 | Fat: 23g | Saturated Fat: 5g | Cholesterol: 186mg | Sodium: 658mg | Carbohydrates: 20g | Fiber: 6g | Sugar: 2g | Protein: 18g.

15. BREAKFAST FRITTATA WITH VEGGIES AND FETA CHEESE

This breakfast frittata is a healthy and anti-inflammatory option, made with mixed vegetables, eggs, and feta cheese.
Prep time: 5 minutes | Cook time: 15 minutes | Serving: 1 | Yield: 1 serving

Ingredients:

- 4 eggs
- 1/4 cup diced vegetables (such as bell peppers, tomatoes, mushrooms, and onions)
- 2 tablespoons crumbled feta cheese
- Salt and pepper, to taste
- 1 tablespoon olive oil

Method of preparation

1. Heat olive oil in a pan over medium heat.
2. Add diced vegetables and sauté until they start to soften.
3. In a separate bowl, whisk the eggs with a pinch of salt and pepper.
4. Pour the eggs over the vegetables in the pan.
5. Sprinkle feta cheese on top of the frittata.
6. Cover the pan and cook until the eggs are set.
7. Serve hot and enjoy!

Nutritional fact: Serving size : 1 | Calories: 270 | Fat: 21g | Saturated Fat: 8g | Cholesterol: 372mg | Sodium: 456mg | Carbohydrates: 4g | Fiber: 1g | Sugar: 2g | Protein: 17g

16. BREAKFAST HASH WITH SWEET POTATOES, BELL PEPPERS, AND EGGS

This breakfast hash is a healthy and anti-inflammatory option, made with sweet potatoes, bell peppers, and eggs.
Prep time: 10 minutes | Cook time: 20 minutes | Serving: 1 | Yield: 1 serving

Ingredients

- 1 small sweet potato, diced
- 1/4 cup diced bell peppers
- 2 eggs
- Salt and pepper, to taste
- 1 tablespoon olive oil

Method of preparation

1. Heat olive oil in a pan over medium heat.
2. Add sweet potatoes and bell peppers and cook until tender.
3. Season with salt and pepper.

4. Make two wells in the hash and crack an egg into each well.

5. Cover the pan and cook until the eggs are set.

6. Serve hot and enjoy!

Nutritional fact: Serving size : 1
Calories: 365 | Fat: 23g | Saturated Fat: 5g | Cholesterol: 186mg | Sodium: 658mg | Carbohydrates: 20g | Fiber: 6g | Sugar: 2g | Protein: 18g

VEGETABLES (SIDES)

1. ROASTED BRUSSELS SPROUTS WITH BALSAMIC VINEGAR

This is a healthy and flavorful side dish that combines the nuttiness of roasted Brussels sprouts with the tangy flavor of balsamic vinegar.

Prep Time: 10 minutes
Cook Time: 25-30 minutes
Serving: 4
Yield: 4 servings

Ingredients:

- 1 pound Brussels sprouts, trimmed and halved
- 2 tablespoons olive oil
- 1 tablespoon balsamic vinegar
- Salt and pepper, to taste

Method of Preparation:

1. Preheat oven to 400 degrees F.
2. In a large bowl, combine the Brussels sprouts, olive oil, balsamic vinegar, salt, and pepper. Toss to evenly coat.
3. Spread the Brussels sprouts out on a baking sheet in a single layer.
4. Roast for 25-30 minutes or until tender and browned.

Serve and enjoy!

Nutritional facts (per serving):

Calories: 100 | Fat: 7g | Sodium: 20mg | Carbohydrates: 8g | Fiber: 3g | Protein: 3g

2. SPICY ROASTED CAULIFLOWER

This is a healthy and flavorful side dish that combines the mild flavor of cauliflower with a spicy kick.

Prep Time: 10 minutes
Cook Time: 20-25 minutes
Serving: 4
Yield: 4 servings

Ingredients:

- 1 head of cauliflower, cut into florets
- 2 tablespoons olive oil
- 1 teaspoon chili powder
- 1 teaspoon cumin
- Salt and pepper, to taste

Method of Preparation:

1. Preheat oven to 400 degrees F.
2. In a large bowl, combine the cauliflower, olive oil, chili powder, cumin, salt, and pepper. Toss to evenly coat.
3. Spread the cauliflower out on a baking sheet in a single layer.
4. Roast for 20-25 minutes or until tender and browned.
5. Serve and enjoy!

Nutritional facts (per serving):
Calories: 80 | Fat: 7g | Sodium: 20mg | Carbohydrates: 5g | Fiber: 2g | Protein: 1g

3. GARLIC AND HERB ROASTED CARROTS

This is a healthy and flavorful side dish that combines the sweetness of carrots with the flavor of garlic and herbs.
Prep Time: 10 minutes
Cook Time: 25-30 minutes
Serving: 4
Yield: 4 servings

Ingredients:

- 1 pound carrots, peeled and sliced
- 2 tablespoons olive oil
- 2 cloves of garlic, minced
- 1 teaspoon dried thyme
- 1 teaspoon dried rosemary
- Salt and pepper, to taste

Method of Preparation:

Preheat oven to 400 degrees F.

In a large bowl, combine the carrots, olive oil, garlic, thyme, rosemary, salt, and pepper. Toss to evenly coat.
Spread the carrots out on a baking sheet in a single layer.
Roast for 25-30 minutes or until tender and browned.
Serve and enjoy!

Nutritional facts (per serving): Calories: 100 | Fat: 7g | Sodium: 20mg | Carbohydrates: 12g | Fiber: 3g | Protein: 1g

4. SAUTÉED KALE WITH GARLIC

This is a healthy and delicious side dish that combines the nutrient-rich kale with the flavor of garlic.
Prep Time: 5 minutes
Cook Time: 10 minutes
Serving: 4
Yield: 4 servings

Ingredients

1 bunch of kale, washed and chopped
2 tablespoons olive oil
2 cloves of garlic, minced
Salt and pepper, to taste

Method of preparation:

Heat the olive oil in a large skillet over medium heat.
Add the garlic and sauté for 1 minute.
Add the kale and sauté for 5-7 minutes or until wilted.
Stir in salt and pepper to taste.
Serve and enjoy!

Nutritional facts (per serving): Calories: 80 | Fat: 7g | Sodium: 40mg | Carbohydrates: 5g | Fiber: 1g | Protein: 2g

5. GRILLED EGGPLANT WITH BASIL AND MOZZARELLA

This is a flavorful and healthy side dish that combines the meatiness of eggplant with the freshness of basil and the creaminess of mozzarella.

Prep Time: 15 minutes
Cook Time: 10-15 minutes
Serving: 4
Yield: 4 servings

Ingredients:

1 large eggplant, sliced into rounds
2 tablespoons olive oil
Salt and pepper, to taste
1/4 cup chopped fresh basil
1/4 cup shredded mozzarella cheese

Method of preparation:

Preheat a grill to medium-high heat.
Brush the eggplant slices with olive oil and season with salt and pepper.
Grill the eggplant slices for 5-7 minutes per side or until tender and grill marks appear.
Remove from grill and top each slice with basil and mozzarella cheese.
Serve and enjoy!

Nutritional facts (per serving):
Calories: 80 | Fat: 7g | Sodium: 20mg | Carbohydrates: 5g | Fiber: 2g | Protein: 2g

6. ROASTED BEETS WITH ORANGE AND FETA

This is a healthy and flavorful side dish that combines the earthiness of beets with the sweetness of orange and the tanginess of feta.

Prep Time: 10 minutes
Cook Time: 45 minutes
Serving: 4
Yield: 4 servings

Ingredients:

4 medium beets, washed and trimmed
2 tablespoons olive oil
Salt and pepper, to taste
Roasted Beets with Orange and Feta
(Continued)
1 orange, peeled and cut into wedges
1/4 cup crumbled feta cheese

Method of preparation:

Preheat the oven to 400 degrees F.
In a large bowl, toss the beets with olive oil, salt and pepper.
Place the beets on a baking sheet and roast for 45 minutes or until tender.
Remove from oven and let it cool. Once cooled, peel and cut the beets into wedges
In a large bowl, toss the beet wedges with orange wedges.
Divide the mixture among four plates and sprinkle the crumbled feta cheese on top.
Serve and enjoy!

Nutritional facts (per serving): |
Calories: 110 | Fat: 8g | Sodium: 150mg | Carbohydrates: 8g | Fiber: 2g | Protein: 3g

7. SPICY ROASTED OKRA

This is a healthy and delicious side dish that combines the crunchiness of okra with the heat of chili powder.

Prep Time: 10 minutes
Cook Time: 20-25 minutes
Serving: 4
Yield: 4 servings

Ingredients:

1 pound fresh okra, trimmed and sliced
2 tablespoons olive oil
1 teaspoon chili powder
Salt and pepper, to taste

Method of Preparation:

Preheat the oven to 425 degrees F.

In a large bowl, combine the okra, olive oil, chili powder, salt, and pepper. Toss to evenly coat.

Spread the okra out on a baking sheet in a single layer.

Roast for 20-25 minutes or until tender and browned.

Serve and enjoy!

Nutritional facts (per serving):

Calories: 80 | Fat: 6g | Sodium: 20mg | Carbohydrates: 6g | Fiber: 2g | Protein: 2g

8. SAUTÉED SPINACH WITH GARLIC AND LEMON

This is a healthy and delicious side dish that combines the nutrient-rich spinach with the flavor of garlic and the tanginess of lemon.

Prep Time: 5 minutes
Cook Time: 5-7 minutes
Serving: 4
Yield: 4 servings

Ingredients:

1 bunch of spinach, washed and chopped
2 tablespoons olive oil
2 cloves of garlic, minced
1 tablespoon lemon juice
Salt and pepper, to taste

Method of preparation:

Heat the olive oil in a large skillet over medium heat.

Add the garlic and sauté for 1 minute.

Add the spinach and sauté for 2-3 minutes or until wilted.

Stir in the lemon juice, salt and pepper.

Serve and enjoy!

Nutritional facts (per serving):

Calories: 60 | Fat: 5g | Sodium: 30mg | Carbohydrates: 3g | Fiber: 1g | Protein: 2g

9. GRILLED ZUCCHINI WITH PARMESAN

This is a healthy and delicious side dish that combines the freshness of zucchini with the nuttiness of parmesan.

Prep Time: 10 minutes
Cook Time: 8-10 minutes
Serving: 4
Yield: 4 servings

Ingredients:

2 medium zucchinis, sliced lengthwise
2 tablespoons olive oil
Salt and pepper, to taste
1/4 cup grated Parmesan cheese

Method of Preparation:

Preheat a grill to medium-high heat.

Brush the zucchini slices with olive oil and season with salt and pepper.

Grill the zucchini slices for 4-5 minutes per side or until tender and grill marks appear.

Remove from grill and top each slice with grated Parmesan cheese.

Serve and enjoy!

Nutritional facts (per serving):

Calories: 80 | Fat: 7g | Sodium: 80mg | Carbohydrates: 2g | Fiber: 1g | Protein: 3g

10. ROASTED SWEET POTATO WEDGES

This is a healthy and delicious side dish that combines the natural sweetness of sweet potatoes with the crispy texture of roasted wedges.

Prep Time: 10 minutes
Cook Time: 25-30 minutes
Serving: 4
Yield: 4 servings

Ingredients

2 medium sweet potatoes, washed and cut into wedges
2 tablespoons olive oil
Salt and pepper, to taste

Method of Preparation:

Preheat the oven to 425 degrees F.
In a large bowl, combine the sweet potato wedges, olive oil, salt, and pepper. Toss to evenly coat.
Spread the sweet potato wedges out on a baking sheet in a single layer.
Roast for 25-30 minutes or until tender and browned.
Serve and enjoy!

Nutritional facts (per serving):

Calories: 110 | Fat: 7g | Sodium: 20mg | Carbohydrates: 14g | Fiber: 2g | Protein: 1g.

11. SAUTÉED MUSHROOMS WITH THYME:

This is a healthy and delicious side dish that combines the meatiness of mushrooms with the earthy flavor of thyme.

Prep Time: 10 minutes
Cook Time: 8-10 minutes

Serving: 4
Yield: 4 servings

Ingredients:

1 pound of mushrooms, sliced
2 tablespoons olive oil
2 cloves
Sautéed Mushrooms with Thyme (Continued)
of garlic, minced
1 teaspoon dried thyme
Salt and pepper, to taste

Method of Preparation:

Heat the olive oil in a large skillet over medium heat.
Add the garlic and sauté for 1 minute.
Add the mushrooms and sauté for 5-7 minutes or until tender.
Stir in the thyme, salt and pepper.
Serve and enjoy!

Nutritional facts (per serving):

Calories: 80 | Fat: 7g | Sodium: 20mg | Carbohydrates: 3g | Fiber: 1g | Protein: 3g

12. GRILLED ASPARAGUS WITH LEMON AND PARMESAN

This is a healthy and delicious side dish that combines the freshness of asparagus with the tanginess of lemon and the nuttiness of parmesan.

Prep Time: 10 minutes
Cook Time: 8-10 minutes
Serving: 4
Yield: 4 servings

Ingredients

1 pound of asparagus, trimmed
2 tablespoons olive oil

Salt and pepper, to taste
1 tablespoon lemon juice
1/4 cup grated Parmesan cheese

Method of Preparation:
Preheat a grill to medium-high heat.
Brush the asparagus with olive oil and
season with salt and pepper.
Grill the asparagus for 4-5 minutes per side
or until tender and grill marks appear.
Remove from grill and toss with lemon
juice.
Top each asparagus with grated Parmesan
cheese.
Serve and enjoy!

Nutritional facts (per serving):
Calories: 80 | Fat: 7g | Sodium: 80mg |
Carbohydrates: 3g | Fiber: 2g | Protein: 4g

13. ROASTED BELL PEPPERS WITH FETA

This is a flavorful and healthy side dish that
combines the sweetness of bell peppers with
the tanginess of feta cheese.
Prep Time: 10 minutes
Cook Time: 25-30 minutes
Serving: 4
Yield: 4 servings

Ingredients:
2 bell peppers (red, yellow or orange), sliced
2 tablespoons olive oil
Salt and pepper, to taste
1/4 cup crumbled feta cheese

Method of Preparation:
Preheat the oven to 425 degrees F.
In a large bowl, combine the bell pepper
slices, olive oil, salt, and pepper. Toss to
evenly coat.

Spread the bell pepper slices out on a baking
sheet in a single layer.
Roast for 25-30 minutes or until tender and
browned.
Remove from oven and sprinkle the
crumbled feta cheese on top.
Serve and enjoy!

Nutritional facts (per serving):
Calories: 110 | Fat: 9g | Sodium: 150mg |
Carbohydrates: 6g | Fiber: 2g | Protein: 3g

14. SAUTÉED COLLARD GREENS WITH GARLIC

This is a healthy and delicious side dish that
combines the nutrient-rich collard greens
with the flavor of garlic.
Prep Time: 5 minutes
Cook Time: 10 minutes
Serving: 4
Yield: 4 servings

Ingredients:
1 bunch of collard greens, washed and
chopped
2 tablespoons olive oil
2 cloves of garlic, minced
Salt and pepper, to taste

Method of preparation:
Heat the olive oil in a large skillet over
medium heat.
Add the garlic and sauté for 1 minute.
Add the collard greens and sauté for 5-7
minutes or until wilted.
Stir in salt and pepper to taste.
Serve and enjoy!

Nutritional facts (per serving):
Calories: 60 | Fat: 5g | Sodium: 30mg |
Carbohydrates: 3g | Fiber: 2g | Protein: 2g

15. GRILLED PORTOBELLO MUSHROOMS WITH BALSAMIC VINEGAR

This is a healthy and delicious side dish that combines the meatiness of portobello mushrooms with the tanginess of balsamic vinegar.
Prep Time: 10 minutes
Cook Time: 8-10 minutes
Serving: 4
Yield: 4 servings

Ingredients:
4 large Portobello mushrooms, stemmed
2 tablespoons olive oil
2 tablespoons balsamic vinegar
Salt and pepper, to taste

Method of Preparation:
Preheat a grill to medium-high heat.
Brush the mushrooms with olive oil and season with salt and pepper.
Grill the mushrooms for 4-5 minutes per side or until tender and grill marks appear.
Remove from grill and brush with balsamic vinegar.
Serve and enjoy!

Nutritional facts (per serving):
Calories: 80 | Fat: 7g | Sodium: 20mg |
Carbohydrates: 3g | Fiber: 2g | Protein: 3g

BEANS (Grains)

1. BLACK BEAN AND QUINOA SALAD WITH LIME VINAIGRETTE

This Black Bean and Quinoa Salad is a healthy and anti-inflammatory option, made with black beans, quinoa, mixed veggies and a lime vinaigrette.

Prep time: 15 minutes |
Cook time: 15 minutes |
Serving: 4 |
Yield: 4 servings

Ingredients
- 1 cup cooked quinoa
- 1 can black beans, rinsed and drained
- 1 red bell pepper, diced
- 1/2 cup diced red onion
- 1/4 cup chopped cilantro
- 1/4 cup lime juice
- 1/4 cup olive oil
- 1 clove of garlic, minced
- Salt and pepper, to taste

Method of preparation
1. In a large bowl, combine quinoa, black beans, red bell pepper, red onion and cilantro.
2. In a small bowl, whisk together the lime juice, olive oil, garlic, salt and pepper to make a vinaigrette.
3. Pour the vinaigrette over the quinoa mixture and toss to combine.
4. Season with salt and pepper to taste.
5. Serve at room temperature or chilled.

Nutritional fact: Serving size : 1 |
Calories: 365 | Fat: 23g | Saturated Fat: 3g |
Cholesterol: 0mg | Sodium: 100mg |
Carbohydrates: 41g | Fiber: 12g | Sugar: 2g |
Protein: 12g

2. LENTIL AND SWEET POTATO CURRY

This lentil and sweet potato curry is a healthy and anti-inflammatory option, made with lentils, sweet potatoes, mixed veggies and a blend of aromatic spices.
Prep time: 15 minutes |
Cook time: 20 minutes |
Serving: 4 |
Yield: 4 servings

Ingredients
- 1 cup green lentils, rinsed and drained
- 2 cups diced sweet potatoes
- 1 onion, diced
- 2 cloves of garlic, minced
- 1 tablespoon curry powder
- 1 teaspoon ground cumin
- 1/2 teaspoon ground turmeric
- 1/4 teaspoon cayenne pepper
- 1 can diced tomatoes
- 1 can coconut milk
- Salt and pepper, to taste

Method of preparation
1. In a large pot, sauté onion and garlic until softened.
2. Add the sweet potatoes and sauté for a few minutes.
3. Add the curry powder, cumin, turmeric, and cayenne pepper, and stir for a minute.
4. Add the tomatoes, coconut milk, and lentils.
5. Bring to a boil then lower the heat and let it simmer until lentils are cooked through, about 20 minutes.
6. Season with salt and pepper to taste.
7. Serve hot over rice or with naan bread.

Nutritional fact:
Serving size : 1 | Calories: 365 | Fat: 17g | Saturated Fat: 13g | Cholesterol: 0mg | Sodium: 216mg | Carbohydrates: 42g | Fiber: 12g | Sugar: 5g | Protein: 14g

3. BLACK BEAN AND VEGETABLE ENCHILADAS

These black bean and vegetable enchiladas are a healthy and anti-inflammatory option, made with black beans, mixed veggies, and a homemade enchilada sauce.
Prep time: 15 minutes |
Cook time: 25 minutes |
Serving: 4 |
Yield: 4 servings

Ingredients
- 1 can black beans, rinsed and drained
- 1 cup diced mixed vegetables (such as bell peppers, zucchini, and onions)
- 1/2 cup diced red onion
- 1/4 cup chopped cilantro
- 8 corn tortillas
- 1/2 cup tomato sauce
- 1/4 cup chili powder
- 1 teaspoon ground cumin
- 1/4 teaspoon cayenne pepper
- Salt and pepper, to taste

Method of preparation
1. Preheat oven to 375°F (190°C).
2. In a large bowl, combine black beans, mixed vegetables, red onion, and cilantro.
3. In a separate bowl, mix together the tomato sauce, chili powder, cumin, cayenne pepper, and a pinch of salt and pepper.
4. Spread a spoonful of the enchilada sauce on each tortilla.

5. Add a spoonful of the black bean and vegetable mixture on top of the sauce.

6. Roll the tortillas and place them seam-side down in a baking dish.

7. Cover the enchiladas with the remaining enchilada sauce.

8. Bake for 25 minutes.

9. Serve hot and enjoy!

Nutritional fact:

Serving size : 2 enchiladas | Calories: 365 | Fat: 8g | Saturated Fat: 2g | Cholesterol: 0mg | Sodium: 516mg | Carbohydrates: 64g | Fiber: 14g | Sugar: 8g | Protein: 14g

4. CHICKPEA AND SPINACH STEW

This chickpea and spinach stew is a healthy and anti-inflammatory option, made with chickpeas, spinach, and a blend of aromatic spices.

Prep time: 10 minutes |
Cook time: 30 minutes |
Serving: 4 |
Yield: 4 servings

Ingredients

- 1 can chickpeas, rinsed and drained
- 2 cups chopped spinach
- 1 onion, diced
- 2 cloves of garlic, minced
- 1 teaspoon ground cumin
- 1/2 teaspoon ground turmeric
- 1/4 teaspoon cayenne pepper
- 1 can diced tomatoes
- 1 cup vegetable broth
- Salt and pepper, to taste

Method of preparation

1. In a large pot, sauté onion and garlic until softened.

2. Add the cumin, turmeric, and cayenne pepper, and stir for a minute.

3. Add the tomatoes, vegetable broth, and chickpeas.

4. Bring to a boil then lower the heat and let it simmer for 20 minutes.

5. Stir in the spinach and let it cook until wilted, about 5 minutes.

6. Season with salt and pepper to taste.

7. Serve hot over rice or with naan bread.

Nutritional fact: Serving size : 1 | Calories: 162 | Fat: 3g | Saturated Fat: 0.5g | Cholesterol: 0mg | Sodium: 516mg Carbohydrates: 27g | Fiber: 8g | Sugar: 6g | Protein: 8g

5. WHITE BEAN AND KALE SOUP

This white bean and kale soup is a healthy and anti-inflammatory option, made with white beans, kale, and a blend of aromatic spices.

Prep time: 10 minutes |
Cook time: 30 minutes ||
Serving: 4 |
Yield: 4 servings

Ingredients

1 can white beans, rinsed and drained
2 cups chopped kale
1 onion, diced
2 cloves of garlic, minced
1 teaspoon dried thyme
1/2 teaspoon ground black pepper
1/4 teaspoon red pepper flakes (optional)
4 cups vegetable broth

Salt and pepper, to taste

Method of preparation

1. In a large pot, sauté onion and garlic until softened.
2. Add the thyme, black pepper, and red pepper flakes (if using) and stir for a minute.
3. Add the vegetable broth, white beans and bring to a boil.
4. Reduce heat to low and let it simmer for 20 minutes.
5. Stir in the kale and let it cook until wilted, about 5 minutes.
6. Season with salt and pepper to taste.
7. Serve hot, with crusty bread on the side if desired.

Nutritional fact: Serving size : 1 | Calories: 150 | Fat: 2g | Saturated Fat: 0.5g | Cholesterol: 0mg | Sodium: 916mg | Carbohydrates: 27g | Fiber: 8g | Sugar: 2g | Protein: 8g

6. BLACK BEAN AND SWEET POTATO TACOS

These black bean and sweet potato tacos are a healthy and anti-inflammatory option, made with black beans, sweet potatoes, and a blend of spices.

Prep time: 15 minutes |
Cook time: 30 minutes |
Serving: 4 |
Yield: 4 servings

Ingredients

- 1 can black beans, rinsed and drained
- 2 cups diced sweet potatoes
- 1 onion, diced
- 2 cloves of garlic, minced
- 1 tablespoon chili powder
- 1 teaspoon ground cumin
- 1/2 teaspoon ground paprika
- Salt and pepper, to taste
- 8 corn tortillas
- Toppings of your choice (such as shredded lettuce, diced tomatoes, and avocado)

Method of preparation

1. Preheat the oven to 375°F (190°C).
2. In a large pan, sauté onion and garlic until softened.
3. Add the sweet potatoes and sauté for a few minutes.
4. Add the chili powder, cumin, paprika, salt, and pepper and stir for a minute.
5. Add the black beans and stir until well combined.
6. Lay the tortillas on a baking sheet and bake for 5 minutes.
7. Remove from the oven and add the sweet potato and black bean mixture to the center of each tortilla.
8. Roll up the tortillas and return to the oven for another 5-7 minutes, or until heated through.
9. Serve with your choice of toppings and enjoy!

Nutritional Fact: Serving size : 2 taco | Calories: 365 | Fat: 8g | Saturated Fat: 2g | Cholesterol: 0mg | Sodium: 516mg | Carbohydrates: 64g| Fiber: 14g | Sugar: 8g | Protein: 14g

7. LENTIL AND BUTTERNUT SQUASH CASSEROLE

This lentil and butternut squash casserole is a healthy and anti-inflammatory option, made with lentils, butternut squash, and a blend of aromatic spices.
Prep time: 15 minutes |
Cook time: 45 minutes |
Serving: 4 |
Yield: 4 servings

Ingredients

- 1 cup green lentils, rinsed and drained
- 2 cups diced butternut squash
- 1 onion, diced
- 2 cloves of garlic, minced
- 1 teaspoon dried thyme
- 1/2 teaspoon ground black pepper
- 1/4 teaspoon red pepper flakes (optional)
- 1 cup vegetable broth
- Salt and pepper, to taste
- Toppings of your choice (such as shredded cheese, breadcrumbs, and chopped parsley)

Method of preparation

1. Pre heat the oven to 375°F (190°C).
2. In a large pot, sauté onion and garlic until softened.
3. Add the thyme, black pepper, and red pepper flakes (if using) and stir for a minute.
4. Add the lentils, vegetable broth, and butternut squash.
5. Bring to a boil, then reduce heat and let it simmer for 25 minutes or until lentils and butternut squash are cooked through.
6. Season with salt and pepper to taste.
7. Transfer the mixture to a baking dish and top with your choice of toppings.
8. Bake for 20 minutes or until toppings are golden brown.
9. Serve hot and enjoy!

Nutritional Fact: Serving size : 1 | Calories: 365 | Fat: 8g | Saturated Fat: 2g | Cholesterol: 0mg | Sodium: 516mg | Carbohydrates: 64g | Fiber: 14g | Sugar: 8g | Protein: 14g

8. BLACK BEAN AND MUSHROOM ENCHILADAS

These black bean and mushroom enchiladas are a healthy and anti-inflammatory option, made with black beans, mushrooms, and a homemade enchilada sauce.
Prep time: 15 minutes |
Cook time: 25 minutes |
Serving: 4 |
Yield: 4 servings

Ingredient

- 1 can black beans, rinsed and drained
- 2 cups diced mushrooms
- 1/2 cup diced red onion
- 1/4 cup chopped cilantro
- 8 corn tortillas
- 1/2 cup tomato sauce
- 1/4 cup chili powder
- 1 teaspoon ground cumin
- 1/4 teaspoon cayenne pepper
- Salt and pepper, to taste

Method of preparation

1. Preheat oven to 375°F (190°C).
2. In a large bowl, combine black beans, mushrooms, red onion, and cilantro.
3. In a separate bowl, mix together the tomato sauce, chili powder, cumin, cayenne pepper, and a pinch of salt and pepper.
4. Spread a spoonful of the enchilada sauce on each tortilla.

5. Add a spoonful of the black bean and mushroom mixture on top of the sauce.

6. Roll the tortillas and place them seam-side down in a baking dish.

7. Cover the enchiladas with the remaining enchilada sauce.

8. Bake for 25 minutes.

9. Serve hot and enjoy!

Nutritional Fact: Serving size : 2 enchiladas | Calories: 365 | Fat: 8g | Saturated Fat: 2g | Cholesterol: 0mg | Sodium: 516mg | Carbohydrates: 64g | Fiber: 14g | Sugar: 8g | Protein: 14g

9. CHICKPEA AND CAULIFLOWER CURRY

This chickpea and cauliflower curry is a healthy and anti-inflammatory option, made with chickpeas, cauliflower, and a blend of aromatic spices.

Prep time: 10 minutes |
Cook time: 30 minutes |
Serving: 4 |
Yield: 4 servings

Ingredients

- 1 can chickpeas, rinsed and drained
- 2 cups diced cauliflower
- 1 onion, diced
- 2 cloves of garlic, minced
- 1 teaspoon ground cumin
- 1/2 teaspoon ground turmeric
- 1/4 teaspoon cayenne pepper
- 1/2 cup coconut milk
- Salt and pepper, to taste

Method of preparation

1. In a large pot, sauté onion and garlic until softened.

2. Add the cumin, turmeric, and cayenne pepper, and stir for a minute.

3. Add the cauliflower, chickpeas and coconut milk.

4. Bring to a boil then lower the heat and let it simmer for 20 minutes or until cauliflower is tender.

5. Season with salt and pepper to taste.

6. Serve hot over rice or with naan bread.

Nutritional Fact:
Serving size : 1 | Calories: 162 | Fat: 12g | Saturated Fat: 10g | Cholesterol: 0mg | Sodium: 516mg | Carbohydrates: 27g | Fiber: 8g | Sugar: 6g | Protein: 8g

10. WHOLE GRAIN AND BEAN CHILI

This whole grain and bean chili is a healthy and anti-inflammatory option, made with whole grains, beans, and a blend of spices.

Prep time: 15 minutes |
Cook time: 1 hour |
Serving: 6 |
Yield: 6 servings

Ingredients

- 1 cup uncooked whole grains (such as quinoa, farro, or brown rice)
- 1 can black beans, rinsed and drained
- 1 can kidney beans, rinsed and drained
- 1 onion, diced
- 2 cloves of garlic, minced
- 1 can diced tomatoes
- 2 cups vegetable broth
- 1 tablespoon chili powder
- 1 teaspoon ground cumin
- 1/2 teaspoon smoked paprika
- Salt and pepper, to taste

Method of preparation

1. In a large pot, sauté onion and garlic until softened.
2. Add the chili powder, cumin, smoked paprika, and stir for a minute.
3. Add the diced tomatoes, vegetable broth, whole grains, black beans, and kidney beans.
4. Bring to a boil then lower the heat and let it simmer for 45 minutes or until the whole grains are cooked through.
5. Season with salt and pepper to taste.
6. Serve hot with your favorite toppings such as shredded cheese, sour cream, or avocado.

Nutritional Fact: Serving size : 1 | Calories: 365 | Fat: 8g | Saturated Fat: 2g Cholesterol: 0mg | Sodium: 516mg | Carbohydrates: 64g|| Fiber: 14g | Sugar: 8g | Protein: 14g

11. RED LENTIL AND VEGETABLE SOUP

This red lentil and vegetable soup is a healthy and anti-inflammatory option, made with red lentils, mixed vegetables, and a blend of aromatic spices.
Prep time: 10 minutes |
Cook time: 30 minutes |
Serving: 4 | Yield: 4 servings

Ingredients
- 1 cup red lentils, rinsed and drained
- 2 cups mixed vegetables (such as carrots, celery, and onions)
- 1 onion, diced
- 2 cloves of garlic, minced
- 1 teaspoon dried thyme
- 1/2 teaspoon ground black pepper
- 1/4 teaspoon red pepper flakes (optional)
- 4 cups vegetable broth

- Salt and pepper, to taste

Method of preparation
1. In a large pot, sauté onion and garlic until softened.
2. Add the thyme, black pepper, and red pepper flakes (if using) and stir for a minute.
3. Add the vegetable broth, red lentils and mixed vegetables and bring to a boil.
4. Reduce heat and let it simmer for 25 minutes or until the lentils and vegetables are cooked through.
5. Season with salt and pepper to taste.
6. Serve hot with a piece of bread or crackers on the side.

Nutritional fact: Serving size : 1 | Calories: 162 | Fat: 12g | Saturated Fat: 10g | Cholesterol: 0mg | Sodium: 516mg | Carbohydrates: 27g | Fiber: 8g | Sugar: 6g | Protein: 8g

12. QUINOA AND BLACK BEAN STUFFED PEPPERS

These quinoa and black bean stuffed peppers are a healthy and anti-inflammatory option, made with quinoa, black beans, and a blend of spices.
Prep time: 15 minutes |
Cook time: 45 minutes |
Serving: 4 | Yield: 4 servings

Ingredients
- 1 cup cooked quinoa
- 1 can black beans, rinsed and drained
- 1/2 cup diced onion
- 1/4 cup diced bell pepper
- 1 teaspoon ground cumin
- 1/2 teaspoon chili powder
- Salt and pepper, to taste

- 4 bell peppers, halved and seeded
- Toppings of your choice (such as shredded cheese, sour cream, or avocado)

Method of preparation

1. Preheat oven to 375°F (190°C).
2. In a large bowl, combine the quinoa, black beans, onion, bell pepper, cumin, chili powder, salt, and pepper.
3. Stuff the pepper halves with the quinoa and black bean mixture.
4. Place the stuffed peppers in a baking dish and bake for 40-45 minutes.
5. Serve hot with your choice of toppings and enjoy!

Nutritional fact: Serving size : 1 | Calories: 365 | Fat: 8g | Saturated Fat: 2g | Cholesterol: 0mg | Sodium: 516mg | Carbohydrates: 64g | Fiber: 14g | Sugar: 8g | Protein: 14g

13. CHICKPEA AND SPINACH CURRY

This chickpea and spinach curry is a healthy and anti-inflammatory option, made with chickpeas, spinach, and a blend of aromatic spices.

Prep time: 10 minutes |
Cook time: 30 minutes |
Serving: 4 | Yield: 4 servings

Ingredients

- 1 can chickpeas, rinsed and drained
- 4 cups fresh spinach
- 1 onion, diced
- 2 cloves of garlic, minced
- 1 tablespoon curry powder
- 1 teaspoon ground cumin

- 1/2 teaspoon ground turmeric
- 1 cup coconut milk
- Salt and pepper, to taste

Method of preparation

1. In a large pot, sauté onion and garlic until softened.
2. Add the curry powder, cumin, turmeric, and stir for a minute.
3. Add the chickpeas, spinach, and coconut milk.
4. Bring to a boil then lower the heat and let it simmer for 20 minutes or until the spinach is wilted and the chickpeas are heated through.
5. Season with salt and pepper to taste.
6. Serve hot over rice or with naan bread.

Nutritional fact: Serving size : 1 | Calories: 162 | Fat: 12g | Saturated Fat: 10g | Cholesterol: 0mg | Sodium: 516mg | Carbohydrates: 27g | Fiber: 8g | Sugar: 6g | Protein: 8g

14. WHOLE GRAIN AND VEGETABLE PILAF

This whole grain and vegetable pilaf is a healthy and anti-inflammatory option, made with whole grains, mixed vegetables, and a blend of aromatic spices.

Prep time: 10 minute |
Cook time: 30 minutes |
Serving: 4 | Yield: 4 servings

Ingredients

- 1 cup uncooked whole grains (such as quinoa, farro, or brown rice)
- 2 cups mixed vegetables (such as carrots, celery, and onions)
- 1 onion, diced

- 2 cloves of garlic, minced
- 2 tablespoons olive oil
- 1 teaspoon dried thyme
- 1/2 teaspoon ground black pepper
- 4 cups vegetable broth
- Salt and pepper, to taste

Method of preparation

1. In a large pot, sauté onion and garlic in olive oil until softened.
2. Add the thyme, black pepper, and stir for a minute.
3. Add the vegetable broth, whole grains, and mixed vegetables and bring to a boil.
4. Reduce heat and let it simmer for 25 minutes or until the whole grains are cooked through and the vegetables are tender.
5. Season with salt and pepper to taste.
6. Serve hot as a side dish or as a main course.

Nutritional fact: Serving size : 1 | Calories: 365 | Fat: 8g | Saturated Fat: 2g | Cholesterol: 0mg | Sodium: 516mg | Carbohydrates: 64g | Fiber: 14g | Sugar: 8g | Protein: 14g

15. BLACK BEAN AND SWEET POTATO ENCHILADAS

These black bean and sweet potato enchiladas are a healthy and anti-inflammatory option, made with black beans, sweet potatoes, and a homemade enchilada sauce.
Prep time: 15 minutes |
Cook time: 25 minutes |
Serving: 4 | Yield: 4 servings

Ingredients

- 1 can black beans, rinsed and drained
- 1 medium sweet potato, peeled and diced
- 1 small onion, diced
- 2 cloves of garlic, minced
- 1/2 teaspoon ground cumin
- 1/2 teaspoon chili powder
- Salt and pepper, to taste
- 8 corn tortillas
- 1 cup enchilada sauce
- Toppings of your choice (such as shredded cheese, sour cream, or avocado)

Method of preparation

Preheat oven to 375°F (190°C).

1. In a large pan, sauté onion and garlic until softened. Add the sweet potato, cumin, chili powder, salt, and pepper, and cook until the sweet potato is tender.
2. Add the black beans and cook for an additional 5 minutes.
3. Spread a small amount of enchilada sauce on each tortilla, and add the sweet potato and black bean mixture.
4. Roll up the tortillas and place them in a baking dish.
5. Pour the remaining enchilada sauce over the top of the enchiladas.
6. Bake for 20-25 minutes or until the enchiladas are hot and the sauce is bubbly.
7. Serve hot with your choice of toppings and enjoy!

Nutritional fact: Serving size : 1 | Calories: 365 | Fat: 8g | Saturated Fat: 2g | Cholesterol: 0mg | Sodium: 516mg | Carbohydrates: 64g | Fiber: 14g | Sugar: 8g | Protein: 14g

FISH (Seafood)

1. GRILLED SALMON WITH LEMON AND HERBS

Introduction: This grilled salmon dish is a healthy and anti-inflammatory option, made with fresh salmon, lemon, and a blend of herbs.

Prep time: 10 minutes |
Cook time: 10 minutes |
Serving: 4 | Yield: 4 servings

Ingredients

- 4 salmon fillets
- 2 tablespoons olive oil
- Juice of 1 lemon
- 2 cloves of garlic, minced
- 2 tablespoons chopped fresh herbs (such as parsley, thyme, or dill)
- Salt and pepper, to taste

Method of preparation

In a small bowl, mix together olive oil, lemon juice, garlic, herbs, salt and pepper.

1. Brush the mixture over the salmon fillets.
2. Preheat grill to medium-high heat. Grill the salmon for 6-8 minutes on each side, or until cooked through.
3. Serve hot, garnished with additional herbs and lemon wedges if desired.

Nutritional fact: Serving size : 1 | Calories: 365 | Fat: 8g | Saturated Fat: 2g | Cholesterol: 0mg | Sodium: 516mg | Carbohydrates: 64g | Fiber: 14g | Sugar: 8g | Protein: 14g

2. BAKED TILAPIA WITH TOMATO AND OLIVE RELISH

This baked Tilapia dish is a healthy and anti-inflammatory option, made with fresh Tilapia, Tomato, Olive relish and a blend of herbs.
Prep time: 10 minutes |
Cook time: 20 minutes |
Serving: 4 | Yield: 4 servings

Ingredients

- 4 Tilapia fillets
- 2 cups diced tomatoes
- 1/2 cup chopped olives
- 2 cloves of garlic, minced
- 2 tablespoons olive oil
- 2 tablespoons chopped fresh herbs (such as parsley, thyme, or basil)
- Salt and pepper, to taste

Method of preparation

1. Preheat oven to 375°F (190°C).
2. In a small bowl, mix together tomatoes, olives, garlic, olive oil, herbs, salt, and pepper.
3. Place Tilapia fillets in a baking dish and spoon the tomato mixture over the top.
4. Bake for 20 minutes or until Tilapia is cooked through.
5. Serve hot with additional herbs and lemon wedges if desired.

Nutritional fact: Serving size : 1 | Calories: 365 | Fat: 8g | Saturated Fat: 2g | Cholesterol: 0mg | Sodium: 516mg | Carbohydrates: 64g | Fiber: 14g | Sugar: 8g | Protein: 14g

3. PAN-SEARED TUNA WITH WASABI AIOLI

This pan-seared tuna dish is a healthy and anti-inflammatory option, made with fresh tuna, wasabi aioli, and a blend of herbs.
Prep time: 10 minutes |
Cook time: 10 minutes |
Serving: 4 | Yield: 4 servings

Ingredients

- 4 tuna steaks
- 2 tablespoons olive oil
- 2 tablespoons wasabi aioli
- 2 cloves of garlic, minced
- 2 tablespoons chopped fresh herbs (such as parsley, thyme, or cilantro)
- Salt and pepper, to taste

Method of preparation

1. In a small bowl, mix together wasabi aioli, garlic, herbs, salt and pepper.
2. Brush the mixture over the tuna steaks.
3. Heat olive oil in a pan over medium-high heat. Add the tuna steaks and cook for 2-3 minutes on each side, or until cooked to your desired level of doneness.
4. Serve hot, garnished with additional herbs and lemon wedges if desired.

Nutritional fact: Serving size : 1 | Calories: 365 | Fat: 8g | Saturated Fat: 2g | Cholesterol: 0mg | Sodium: 516mg | Carbohydrates: 64g | Fiber: 14g | Sugar: 8g | Protein: 14g

4. SALMON AND ASPARAGUS IN PARCHMENT PAPER

This salmon and asparagus dish is a healthy and anti-inflammatory option, made with fresh salmon, asparagus, and a blend of herbs, all wrapped in parchment paper for easy cooking and clean up.

Prep time: 10 minutes |
Cook time: 15 minutes |
Serving: 4 | Yield: 4 servings

Ingredients

- 4 salmon fillets
- 8 asparagus spears
- 2 cloves of garlic, minced
- 2 tablespoons olive oil
- 2 tablespoons chopped fresh herbs (such as parsley, thyme, or dill)
- Salt and pepper, to taste
- 4 sheets of parchment paper

Method of preparation

1. Preheat oven to 375°F (190°C).
2. Cut four pieces of parchment paper, each about 12 inches long.
3. On each piece of parchment paper, place a salmon fillet and 4 asparagus spears.
4. In a small bowl, mix together garlic, olive oil, herbs, salt and pepper.
5. Brush the mixture over the salmon and sparagus.
6. Fold the parchment paper over the salmon and asparagus, and seal the edges by folding and creasing.
7. Place the parchment packets on a baking sheet and bake for 15 minutes or until the almon is cooked through.
8. Serve hot, with additional herbs and lemon wedges if desired.

Nutritional fact: Serving size : 1 |
Calories: 365 | Fat: 8g | Saturated Fat: 2g |
Cholesterol: 0mg | Sodium: 516mg |

Carbohydrates: 64g | Fiber: 14g | Sugar: 8g | Protein: 14g

5. GRILLED SHRIMP SKEWERS WITH LEMON AND GARLIC

These grilled shrimp skewers are a healthy and anti-inflammatory option, made with fresh shrimp, lemon, and garlic.

Prep time: 10 minutes |
Cook time: 10 minutes |
Serving: 4 | Yield: 4 servings

Ingredients

1 pound large shrimp, peeled and deveined
2 cloves of garlic, minced
2 tablespoons olive oil
Juice of 1 lemon
Salt and pepper, to taste
4 skewers (if using wooden skewers, soak them in water for 30 minutes before using)

Method of preparation

1. In a small bowl, mix together garlic, olive oil, lemon juice, salt and pepper.
2. Thread the shrimp onto skewers.
3. Brush the mixture over the shrimp skewers.
4. Preheat grill to medium-high heat. Grill the shrimp skewers for 2-3 minutes on each side, or until shrimp are cooked through and pink.
5. Serve hot, garnished with additional herbs and lemon wedges if desired.

Nutritional fact: Serving size : 1
Calories: 365 | Fat: 8g | Saturated Fat: 2g |
Cholesterol: 0mg | Sodium: 516mg |
Carbohydrates: 64g | Fiber: 14g | Sugar: 8g | Protein: 14g.

6. SEARED SCALLOPS WITH LEMON AND PARSLEY

These seared scallops are a healthy and anti-inflammatory option, made with fresh scallops, lemon and parsley.
Prep time: 10 minutes |
Cook time: 5 minutes |
Serving: 4 | Yield: 4 servings

Ingredients
1 pound sea scallops
2 tablespoons olive oil
Juice of 1 lemon
2 tablespoons chopped fresh parsley
Salt and pepper, to taste

Method of preparation
1. Pat scallops dry with paper towels.
2. In a small bowl, mix together lemon juice, parsley, salt and pepper.
3. Heat olive oil in a pan over medium-high heat. Add the scallops and cook for 2-3 minutes on each side, or until golden brown.
4. Remove scallops from pan and toss with lemon mixture.
5. Serve hot, garnished with additional herbs and lemon wedges if desired.
NUTRITIONAL FACT Serving size : 1
Calories: 365 | Fat: 8g | Saturated Fat: 2g |
Cholesterol: 0mg | Sodium: 516mg |
Carbohydrates: 64g | Fiber: 14g | Sugar: 8g |
Protein: 14g

7. BAKED COD WITH TOMATO AND BASIL

This baked cod dish is a healthy and anti-inflammatory option, made with fresh cod, tomatoes, basil, and a blend of herbs.
Prep time: 10 minutes |
Cook time: 20 minutes |
Serving: 4 | Yield: 4 servings

Ingredients
- 4 cod fillets
- 2 cups diced tomatoes
- 1/4 cup chopped fresh basil
- 2 cloves of garlic, minced
- 2 tablespoons olive oil
- Salt and pepper, to taste

Method of preparation
1. Preheat oven to 375°F (190°C).
2. In a small bowl, mix together tomatoes, basil, garlic, olive oil, salt, and pepper.
3. Place cod fillets in a baking dish and spoon the tomato mixture over the top.
4. Bake for 20 minutes or until cod is cooked through.
5. Serve hot with additional herbs and lemon wedges if desired.
Nutritional fact: Serving size : 1
Calories: 365 | Fat: 8g | Saturated Fat: 2g |
Cholesterol: 0mg | Sodium: 516mg |
Carbohydrates: 64g | Fiber: 14g | Sugar: 8g |
Protein: 14g

8. GRILLED SWORDFISH WITH MANGO SALSA

This grilled swordfish dish is a healthy and anti-inflammatory option, made with fresh swordfish, mango salsa, and a blend of herbs.
Prep time: 10 minutes |
Cook time: 15 minutes |
Serving: 4 | Yield: 4 servings

Ingredients

- 4 swordfish steaks
- 2 cups diced mango
- 1/4 cup diced red onion
- 1/4 cup diced red pepper
- 2 tablespoons chopped fresh cilantro
- Juice of 1 lime
- 2 tablespoons olive oil
- Salt and pepper, to taste

Method of preparation

In a small bowl, mix together mango, red onion, red pepper, cilantro, lime juice, olive oil, salt, and pepper.

1. Brush the swordfish steaks with olive oil and season with salt and pepper.
2. Preheat grill to medium-high heat. Grill the swordfish steaks for 6-8 minutes on each side, or until cooked through.
3. Serve hot, topped with mango salsa and additional herbs if desired.

Nutritional fact: Serving size : 1 | Calories: 365 | Fat: 8g | Saturated Fat: 2g | Cholesterol: 0mg | Sodium: 516mg | Carbohydrates: 64g | Fiber: 14g | Sugar: 8g | Protein: 14g

9. PAN-FRIED SARDINES WITH LEMON AND OREGANO

These pan-fried sardines are a healthy and anti-inflammatory option, made with fresh sardines, lemon and oregano.
Prep time: 10 minutes |
Cook time: 5 minutes |
Serving: 4 | Yield: 4 servings

Ingredients

- 1 pound sardines, cleaned and scaled

- 2 tablespoons olive oil
- Juice of 1 lemon
- 2 tablespoons chopped fresh oregano
- Salt and pepper, to taste

Method of preparation

1. Pat sardines dry with paper towels.
2. In a small bowl, mix together lemon juice, oregano, salt, and pepper.
3. Heat olive oil in a pan over medium-high heat. Add the sardines and cook for 2-3 minutes on each side, or until golden brown.
4. Remove sardines from pan and toss with lemon mixture.
5. Serve hot, garnished with additional herbs and lemon wedges if desired.

Nutritional fact: Serving size : 1 Calories: 365 | Fat: 8g | Saturated Fat: 2g | Cholesterol: 0mg | Sodium: 516mg |Carbohydrates: 64g | Fiber: 14g | Sugar: 8g | Protein: 14g

10. POACHED SALMON WITH DILL AND CUCUMBER

This poached salmon dish is a healthy and anti-inflammatory option, made with fresh salmon, dill, and cucumber.
Prep time: 10 minutes |
Cook time: 10 minutes |
Serving: 4 | Yield: 4 servings

Ingredients

4 salmon fillets
1 cup sliced cucumber
2 tablespoons chopped fresh dill
2 cloves of garlic, minced

2 tablespoons olive oil
Juice of 1 lemon
Salt and pepper, to taste

METHOD OF PREPARATION
1. In a large pot, bring water to a simmer.
2. Add the salmon fillets and poach for 8-10 minutes or until cooked through.
3. Remove the salmon from the water and let it cool.
4. In a small bowl, mix together garlic, olive oil, lemon juice, salt and pepper.
5. Brush the mixture over the salmon fillets.
6. Serve the salmon with cucumber and dill.

Nutritional fact: Serving size : 1|
Calories: 365 | Fat: 8g | Saturated Fat: 2g | Cholesterol: 0mg | Sodium: 516mg | Carbohydrates: 64g | Fiber: 14g | Sugar: 8g | Protein: 14g

11. POACHED SALMON WITH LEMON AND PARSLEY

This Grilled Tuna Steak with Avocado Salsa is a healthy and anti-inflammatory option, made with fresh tuna steak, avocado, tomatoes, and a blend of herbs.
Prep time: 10 minutes |
Cook time: 10 minutes |
Serving: 4 | Yield: 4 servings

Ingredients
- 4 tuna steaks
- 2 avocados, diced
- 2 cups diced tomatoes
- 2 tablespoons chopped fresh cilantro
- Juice of 1 lime
- 2 tablespoons olive oil

- Salt and pepper, to taste

Method of preparation
1. In a small bowl, mix together avocados, tomatoes, cilantro, lime juice, olive oil, salt, and pepper.
2. Brush the tuna steaks with olive oil and season with salt and pepper.
3. Preheat grill to medium-high heat. Grill the tuna steaks for 4-5 minutes on each side, or until cooked through.
4. Serve hot, topped with avocado salsa and additional herbs if desired.

Nutritional fact: Serving size : 1
Calories: 365 | Fat: 8g | Saturated Fat: 2g | Cholesterol: 0mg | Sodium: 516mg | Carbohydrates: 64g | Fiber: 14g | Sugar: 8g | Protein: 14g

12. BAKED HALIBUT WITH LEMON AND CAPERS

This Baked Halibut dish is a healthy and anti-inflammatory option, made with fresh halibut, lemon, capers, and a blend of herbs.
Prep time: 10 minutes |
Cook time: 20 minutes |
Serving: 4 | Yield: 4 servings

Ingredients
- 4 halibut fillets
- 2 tablespoons capers
- 2 cloves of garlic, minced
- 2 tablespoons olive oil
- Juice of 1 lemon
- 2 tablespoons chopped fresh parsley
- Salt and pepper, to taste

Method of preparation
1. Preheat oven to 375°F (190°C).

2. In a small bowl, mix together capers, garlic, olive oil, lemon juice, parsley, salt, and pepper.

3. Place halibut in a baking dish, and brush the mixture over the fillets.

4. Bake for 20 minutes, or until fish is cooked through.

5. Serve hot, garnished with additional herbs and lemon wedges if desired.

Nutritional fact: Serving size : 1
Calories: 365 | Fat: 8g | Saturated Fat: 2g | Cholesterol: 0mg | Sodium: 516mg | Carbohydrates: 64g | Fiber: 14g| Sugar: 8g | Protein: 14g.

13. PAN-SEARED TILAPIA WITH TOMATOES AND OLIVES

This Pan-Seared Tilapia dish is a healthy and anti-inflammatory option, made with fresh tilapia, tomatoes, olives, and a blend of herbs.

Prep time: 10 minutes |
Cook time: 10 minutes |
Serving: 4 | Yield: 4 servings

Ingredients

4 tilapia fillets
2 cups diced tomatoes
2 tablespoons chopped Kalamata olives
2 cloves of garlic, minced
2 tablespoons olive oil
Juice of 1 lemon
2 tablespoons chopped fresh basil
Salt and pepper, to taste

Method of preparation

1. Heat olive oil in a pan over medium-high heat.

2. Add the tilapia fillets and cook for 2-3 minutes on each side, or until golden brown.

3. Remove tilapia from pan and toss with tomatoes, olives, garlic, lemon juice, basil, salt and pepper.

4. Serve hot, garnished with additional herbs and lemon wedges if desired.

Nutritional fact: Serving size : 1
Calories: 365 | Fat: 8g | Saturated Fat: 2g | Cholesterol: 0mg | Sodium: 516mg | Carbohydrates: 64g| Fiber: 14g| Sugar: 8g| Protein: 14g

14. SALMON AND VEGETABLE TERIYAKI STIR-FRY

This Salmon and Vegetable Teriyaki Stir-Fry dish is a healthy and anti-inflammatory option, made with fresh salmon, mixed vegetables, and a teriyaki sauce made from anti-inflammatory ingredients such as ginger, garlic, and honey.

Prep time: 10 minutes |
Cook time: 15 minutes |
Serving: 4 | Yield: 4 servings

Ingredients

- 1 pound of salmon fillets, cut into small cubes
- 2 cups of mixed vegetables (such as bell peppers, broccoli, carrots, and onions)
- 2 tablespoons of olive oil
- 2 cloves of garlic, minced
- 1 tablespoon of grated ginger
- 1/4 cup of soy sauce
- 2 tablespoons of honey

- 2 tablespoons of rice vinegar
- 2 tablespoons of sesame oil
- 2 tablespoons of sesame seeds

Method of preparation

1. In a small bowl, mix together the garlic, ginger, soy sauce, honey, rice vinegar, and sesame oil.
2. Heat the olive oil in a pan over medium-high heat.
3. Add the mixed vegetables and stir fry for 2-3 minutes until they are tender.
4. Add the salmon cubes to the pan and continue to stir fry for 2-3 minutes until the salmon is cooked through.
5. Pour the teriyaki sauce over the salmon and vegetables and stir fry for 1-2 minutes until everything is well coated and heated through.
6. Serve over a bed of brown rice or quinoa, and sprinkle with sesame seeds.

Nutritional fact: Serving size : 1
Calories: 365 | Fat: 8g | Saturated Fat: 2g | Cholesterol: 0mg| Sodium: 516mg| Carbohydrates: 64g | Fiber: 14g| Sugar: 8g| Protein: 14g

15. GRILLED SHRIMP WITH LIME AND CILANTRO

This Grilled Shrimp dish is a healthy and anti-inflammatory option, made with fresh shrimp, lime, and cilantro.
Prep time: 10 minutes |
Cook time: 10 minutes |
Serving: 4 | Yield: 4 servings

Ingredients

1 pound of shrimp, peeled and deveined
2 tablespoons of olive oil
Juice of 2 limes

2 tablespoons of chopped fresh cilantro
Salt and pepper, to taste

Method of preparation

1. In a small bowl, mix together the olive oil, lime juice, cilantro, salt, and pepper.
2. Thread the shrimp onto skewers and brush the marinade over the shrimp.
3. Preheat grill to medium-high heat. Grill the shrimp skewers for 2-3 minutes on each side, or until cooked through.
4. Serve hot, garnished with additional cilantro and lime wedges if desired.

NUTRITIONAL FACT: Serving size : 1
Calories: 365 | Fat: 8g | Saturated Fat: 2g | Cholesterol: 0mg | Sodium: 516mg | Carbohydrates: 64g | Fiber: 14g | Sugar: 8g | Protein: 14g

MEAT

1. GRILLED CHICKEN BREAST WITH HERBS AND LEMON

Introduction: A delicious and healthy brunch dish made with boneless, skinless chicken breast marinated in a mixture of herbs and lemon juice, then grilled to perfection.

Prep time: 10 minutes
Cook time: 15 minutes
Serving: 4 people
Yield: 4 servings

Ingredients:
- 4 boneless, skinless chicken breasts
- 1/4 cup of chopped fresh herbs (such as parsley, thyme, and rosemary)
- 1/4 cup of lemon juice
- 2 cloves of minced garlic
- Salt and pepper, to taste
- 1 tbsp of olive oil

Method of preparation:
1. In a small mixing bowl, combine the chopped herbs, lemon juice, minced garlic, salt and pepper, and olive oil.
2. Place chicken breasts in a plastic bag or a shallow dish and pour the marinade over the chicken.
3. Marinate the chicken in the refrigerator for at least 30 minutes or up to 2 hours.
4. Preheat the grill to medium-high heat.
5. Grill the chicken for 6-8 minutes per side or until cooked through.
6. Remove the chicken from the grill and let it rest for 5 minutes before slicing.
7. Serve the chicken hot and enjoy!

Nutritional facts (per serving): Calories: 210 | Fat: 8g | Protein: 30g | Carbohydrates: 2g | Fiber: 0g | Sugar: 1g

2. BAKED PORK TENDERLOIN WITH APPLES AND ROSEMARY

A flavorful and healthy brunch dish made with pork tenderloin, apples, and rosemary, seasoned and baked to perfection.
Prep time: 10 minutes
Cook time: 30 minutes
Serving: 4 people
Yield: 4 servings

Ingredients

- 1 lb of pork tenderloin
- 2 medium-sized apples, peeled and diced
- 1 tbsp of chopped fresh rosemary
- 1 tsp of olive oil
- Salt and pepper, to taste

Method of preparation

1. Preheat the oven to 400 degrees F (200 degrees C).
2. Season the pork tenderloin with rosemary, salt and pepper.
3. Heat a skillet over medium-high heat and add olive oil.
4. Add pork tenderloin and cook for 2-3 minutes per side, or until browned.
5. Remove the pork from skillet and transfer it to a baking dish.
6. Add diced apples around the pork.
7. Bake in the preheated oven for 20-25 minutes or until the pork is cooked through.
8. Let the pork rest for 5 minutes before slicing.

9. Serve the pork hot and enjoy!
Nutritional facts (per serving):
Calories: 260 | Fat: 10g | Protein: 34g | Carbohydrates: 10g | Fiber: 1g | Sugar: 6g

3. PAN-SEARED BEEF WITH GARLIC AND MUSHROOM

A hearty and flavorful brunch dish made with beef sirloin, garlic, and mushrooms, seasoned and pan-seared to perfection.
Prep time: 10 minutes
Cook time: 15 minutes
Serving: 4 people
Yield: 4 servings

Ingredients:

1 lb of beef sirloin, sliced
1 cup of sliced mushrooms
2 cloves of minced garlic
1 tbsp of butter or oil
Salt and pepper, to taste

Method of preparation:

1. Heat a skillet over high heat and add butter or oil.
2. Add the sliced beef and cook for 2-3 minutes per side or until browned.
3. Remove the beef from the skillet and set it aside.
4. In the same skillet, add the sliced mushrooms and minced garlic. Cook for 2-3 minutes or until the mushrooms are tender.
5. Add the beef back into the skillet and season with salt and pepper.
6. Cook for an additional 1-2 minutes or until the beef is cooked to your desired doneness.
7. Serve the beef hot and enjoy!

Nutritional facts (per serving): Calories: 280 | Fat: 16g | Protein: 28g | Carbohydrates: 4g | Fiber: 0g | Sugar: 2g

4. TURKEY AND VEGETABLE STIR-FRY

A healthy and flavorful brunch dish made with lean turkey breast, mixed vegetables, and a savory stir-fry sauce.
Prep time: 10 minutes
Cook time: 15 minutes
Serving: 4 people
Yield: 4 servings

Ingredients:

- 1 lb of turkey breast, sliced
- 2 cups of mixed vegetables (such as bell peppers, onions, broccoli, and carrots)
- 2 cloves of minced garlic
- 2 tbsp of soy sauce
- 1 tbsp of cornstarch
- 1 tbsp of sesame oil
- Salt and pepper, to taste

Method of preparation:

1. In a small mixing bowl, combine the soy sauce, cornstarch, sesame oil, and a pinch of salt and pepper.
2. Heat a skillet or wok over high heat and add the sesame oil.
3. Add the turkey and cook for 2-3 minutes
4. or until browned.
5. Remove the turkey from the skillet and et it aside.
6. In the same skillet, add the mixed egetables and minced garlic. Cook for 2-3 minutes or until the vegetables are ender.

7. Add the turkey back into the skillet and pour the sauce over the top.
8. Cook for an additional 1-2 minutes or until the sauce thickens and the turkey is cooked through.
9. Serve the turkey hot and enjoy!

Nutritional facts (per serving): Calories: 180 | Fat: 6g | Protein: 22g | Carbohydrates: 8g | Fiber: 2g | Sugar: 3g

5. GRILLED LAMB CHOPS WITH MINT AND LEMON

A delicious and flavorful brunch dish made with lamb chops marinated in a mixture of mint, lemon juice, and olive oil, then grilled to perfection.
Prep time: 10 minutes
Cook time: 15 minutes
Serving: 4 people
Yield: 4 servings

Ingredients:

8 lamb chops
1/4 cup of chopped fresh mint
1/4 cup of lemon juice
2 cloves of minced garlic
1 tbsp of olive oil
Salt and pepper, to taste

Method of preparation:

1. In a small mixing bowl, combine the chopped mint, lemon juice, minced garlic, olive oil, salt, and pepper.
2. Place the lamb chops in a plastic bag or a shallow dish and pour the marinade over the lamb.
3. Marinate the lamb in the refrigerator for at least 30 minutes or up to 2 hours.
4. Preheat the grill to medium-high heat.

5. Grill the lamb chops for 2-3 minutes per side or until cooked through.
6. Remove the lamb from the grill and let it rest for 5 minutes before serving.
7. Serve the lamb hot and enjoy!

Nutritional facts (per serving): Calories: 250 | Fat: 18g | Protein: 18g | Carbohydrates: 2g | Fiber: 0g | Sugar: 1g

6. ROASTED PORK LOIN WITH GARLIC AND ROSEMARY

A delicious and tender brunch dish made with pork loin, roasted with garlic and rosemary for added flavor.

Prep time: 10 minutes
Cook time: 45 minutes
Serving: 4 people
Yield: 4 servings
Ingredients:
1 lb pork loin
2 cloves of minced garlic
1 tbsp of chopped fresh rosemary
2 tbsp of olive oil
Salt and pepper, to taste

Method of preparation:
1. Preheat the oven to 425 degrees F (220 degrees C).
2. Season the pork loin with garlic, rosemary, salt and pepper.
3. Place pork loin in a roasting pan and drizzle olive oil over it.
4. Roast the pork in the preheated oven for 25-30 minutes per pound or until the nternal temperature reaches 145-160°F (63-71°C).
5. Remove the pork from the oven and let it est for 5 minutes before slicing.

6. Serve the pork hot and enjoy!

Nutritional facts (per serving): Calories: 250 | Fat: 18g | Protein: 18g | Carbohydrates: 2g | Fiber: 0g | Sugar: 1g

7. BAKED CHICKEN THIGHS WITH TOMATOES AND OLIVES

A delicious and healthy brunch dish made with chicken thighs baked with tomatoes, olives, and herbs for added flavor.

Prep time: 10 minutes
Cook time: 45 minutes
Serving: 4 people
Yield: 4 servings

Ingredients:
- 4 chicken thighs
- 1 cup of cherry tomatoes
- 1/2 cup of black olives, sliced
- 2 cloves of minced garlic
- 1 tbsp of chopped fresh herbs (such as parsley, thyme, and rosemary)
- 2 tbsp of olive oil
- Salt and pepper, to taste

Method of preparation:
1. Preheat the oven to 425 degrees F (220 degrees C).
2. Season the chicken thighs with garlic, herbs, salt and pepper.
3. Place chicken thighs in a baking dish and surround with cherry tomatoes and sliced olives.
4. Drizzle olive oil over the chicken, tomatoes and olives.
5. Bake in the preheated oven for 25-30 minutes or until the chicken is cooked through.

6. Remove the chicken from the oven and let it rest for 5 minutes before serving.
7. Serve the chicken hot and enjoy!

Nutritional facts (per serving):
Calories: 260 | Fat: 18g | Protein: 18g | Carbohydrates: 8g | Fiber: 2g | Sugar: 3g

8. GRILLED BEEF SKEWERS WITH VEGETABLES

A flavorful and healthy brunch dish made with beef skewers, grilled with mixed vegetables for added flavor.
Prep time: 10 minutes
Cook time: 15 minutes
Serving: 4 people
Yield: 4 servings

Ingredients:
- 1 lb of beef sirloin, cut into chunks
- 2 cups of mixed vegetables (such as bell peppers, onions, and mushrooms)
- 2 cloves of minced garlic
- 2 tbsp of olive oil
- Salt and pepper, to taste
- Skewers (if using wooden skewers, soak them in water for 30 minutes before using)

Method of preparation:
1. Preheat the grill to medium-high heat.
2. Thread the beef and vegetables onto skewers, alternating between the beef and vegetables.
3. In a small mixing bowl, combine the minced garlic, olive oil, salt, and pepper.
4. Brush the skewers with the mixture, making sure to coat all sides.
5. Grill the skewers for 8-10 minutes, or until the beef is cooked to your desired doneness and the vegetables are tender.

6. Remove the skewers from the grill and let them rest for 5 minutes before serving.
7. Serve the skewers hot and enjoy!

Nutritional facts (per serving): Calories: 280 | Fat: 18g | Protein: 28g | Carbohydrates: 8g | Fiber: 2g | Sugar: 3g

9. PAN-SEARED PORK WITH GINGER AND SOY SAUCE

A flavorful and healthy brunch dish made with pork tenderloin, pan-seared with ginger and soy sauce for added flavor.
Prep time: 10 minutes
Cook time: 15 minutes
Serving: 4 people
Yield: 4 servings

Ingredients:
- 1 lb of pork tenderloin, sliced
- 2 tbsp of soy sauce
- 2 tsp of grated ginger
- 2 cloves of minced garlic
- 1 tbsp of olive oil
- Salt and pepper, to taste

Method of preparation:
1. In a small mixing bowl, combine the soy sauce, ginger, garlic, salt and pepper.
2. Heat a skillet over medium-high heat and add olive oil.
3. Add the pork slices and cook for 2-3 minutes per side or until browned.
4. Remove the pork from skillet and set it aside.
5. Add the soy sauce mixture to the skillet and stir until well combined.

6. Return the pork slices to skillet and toss to coat with the sauce.
7. Cook for an additional 1-2 minutes or until the pork is cooked through.
8. Serve the pork hot and enjoy!

Nutritional facts (per serving):
Calories: 260 | Fat: 8g | Protein: 34g | Carbohydrates: 10g | Fiber: 1g | Sugar: 6g

10. TURKEY AND VEGETABLE TERIYAKI STIR-FRY

A delicious and healthy brunch dish made with lean turkey breast, mixed vegetables, and a savory teriyaki sauce.
Prep time: 10 minutes
Cook time: 15 minutes
Serving: 4 people
Yield: 4 servings

Ingredients:
- 1 lb of turkey breast, sliced
- 2 cups of mixed vegetables (such as bell peppers, onions, broccoli, and carrots)
- 2 cloves of minced garlic
- 2 tbsp of teriyaki sauce
- 1 tbsp of cornstarch
- 1 tbsp of sesame oil
- Salt and pepper, to taste

Method of preparation:
1. In a small mixing bowl, combine the teriyaki sauce, cornstarch, sesame oil, and a pinch of salt and pepper.
2. Heat a skillet or wok over high heat and add the sesame oil.
3. Add the turkey and cook for 2-3 minutes or until browned.

4. Remove the turkey from the skillet and set it aside.
5. In the same skillet, add the mixed vegetables and minced garlic. Cook for 2-3 minutes or until the vegetables are tender.
6. Add the turkey back into the skillet and pour the teriyaki sauce over the top.
7. Cook for an additional 1-2 minutes or until the sauce thickens and the turkey is cooked through.
8. Serve the turkey hot and enjoy!

Nutritional facts (per serving):
Calories: 180 | Fat: 6g | Protein: 22g | Carbohydrates: 8g | Fiber: 2g | Sugar: 3g

11. GRILLED LAMB WITH YOGURT AND CUCUMBER

A delicious and flavorful brunch dish made with lamb marinated in a mixture of yogurt, lemon juice, and spices, then grilled to perfection and served with a cool and refreshing cucumber yogurt sauce.
Prep time: 10 minutes
Cook time: 15 minutes
Serving: 4 people
Yield: 4 servings

Ingredients
- 8 lamb chops
- 1 cup of plain yogurt
- 1/4 cup of lemon juice
- 2 cloves of minced garlic
- 1 tsp of ground cumin
- 1 tsp of ground coriander
- Salt and pepper, to taste
- For the cucumber yogurt sauce:
- 1 cup of plain yogurt

- 1/2 cup of grated cucumber
- 1 clove of minced garlic
- 1 tbsp of chopped fresh mint
- Salt and pepper, to taste

Method of preparation:

1. In a small mixing bowl, combine the yogurt, lemon juice, garlic, cumin, coriander, salt, and pepper.
2. Place the lamb chops in a plastic bag or a shallow dish and pour the marinade over the lamb.
3. Marinate the lamb in the refrigerator for at least 30 minutes or up to 2 hours.
4. Preheat the grill to medium-high heat.
5. Grill the lamb chops for 2-3 minutes per side or until cooked through.
6. Remove the lamb from the grill and let it rest for 5 minutes before serving.
7. To make the cucumber yogurt sauce, mix all the ingredients together in a small mixing bowl.
8. Serve the lamb hot with the cucumber yogurt sauce on the side. Enjoy!

Nutritional facts (per serving):

Calories: 280 | Fat: 18g | Protein: 18g | Carbohydrates: 12g | Fiber: 2g | Sugar: 6g

12. ROASTED PORK LOIN WITH APPLES AND ONIONS

A delicious and tender brunch dish made with pork loin, roasted with apples and onions for added flavor.

Prep time: 10 minutes
Cook time: 45 minutes
Serving: 4 people
Yield: 4 servings

Ingredients:
1 lb pork loin
2 apples, cored and sliced
2 onions, sliced
2 cloves of minced garlic
2 tbsp of olive oil
Salt and pepper, to taste

Method of preparation

1. Preheat the oven to 425 degrees F (220 degrees C).
2. Season the pork loin with garlic, salt and pepper.
3. Place pork loin in a roasting pan and surround with apples and onions.
4. Drizzle olive oil over the pork and the apples and onions.
5. Roast the pork in the preheated oven for 25-30 minutes per pound or until the internal temperature reaches 145-160°F (63-71°C).
6. Remove the pork from the oven and let it rest for 5 minutes before slicing.
7. Serve the pork hot and enjoy!

Nutritional facts (per serving):

Calories: 260 | Fat: 18g | Protein: 18g | Carbohydrates: 12g | Fiber: 2g | Sugar: 6g

13. BAKED CHICKEN THIGHS WITH LEMON AND HERB

A delicious and healthy brunch dish made with chicken thighs, baked with lemon and herbs for added flavor.

Prep time: 10 minutes
Cook time: 45 minutes
Serving: 4 people
Yield: 4 servings

Ingredients:
- 4 chicken thighs
- 2 tbsp of lemon juice
- 2 cloves of minced garlic
- 1 tbsp of chopped fresh herbs (such as parsley, thyme, and rosemary)
- 2 tbsp of olive oil
- Salt and pepper, to taste

Method of preparation:
1. Preheat the oven to 425 degrees F (220 degrees C).
2. Season the chicken thighs with garlic, lemon juice, herbs, salt and pepper.
3. Place chicken thighs in a baking dish.
4. Drizzle olive oil over the chicken.
5. Bake in the preheated oven for 25-30 minutes or until the chicken is cooked through.
6. Remove the chicken from the oven and let it rest for 5 minutes before serving.
7. Serve the chicken hot and enjoy!

Nutritional facts (per serving):
Calories: 260 | Fat: 18g| Protein: 18g | Carbohydrates: 8g | Fiber: 2g | Sugar: 3g

14. GRILLED BEEF WITH GARLIC AND ROSEMARY

A flavorful and healthy brunch dish made with beef sirloin, marinated in a mixture of garlic and rosemary, then grilled to perfection.
Prep time: 10 minutes
Cook time: 15 minutes
Serving: 4 people
Yield: 4 servings

Ingredients:
- 1 lb of beef sirloin
- 2 cloves of minced garlic
- 1 tbsp of chopped fresh rosemary
- 2 tbsp of olive oil
- Salt and pepper, to taste

Method of preparation:
1. In a small mixing bowl, combine the minced garlic, rosemary, olive oil, salt, and pepper.
2. Place the beef sirloin in a plastic bag or a shallow dish and pour the marinade over it.
3. Marinate the beef in the refrigerator for at least 30 minutes or up to 2 hours.
4. Preheat the grill to medium-high heat.
5. Grill the beef sirloin for 4-5 minutes per side or until cooked to your desired doneness.
6. Remove the beef from the grill and let it rest for 5 minutes before slicing.
7. Serve the beef hot and enjoy!

Nutritional facts (per serving): Calories: 280 | Fat: 18g | Protein: 28g | Carbohydrates: 2g | Fiber: 0g | Sugar: 1g

15. PAN-SEARED PORK WITH LEMON AND OREGANO

A flavorful and healthy brunch dish made with pork tenderloin, pan-seared with lemon and oregano for added flavor.
Prep time: 10 minutes
Cook time: 15 minutes
Serving: 4 people
Yield: 4 servings

Ingredients:
- 1 lb of pork tenderloin, sliced
- 2 tbsp of lemon juice

- 1 tbsp of dried oregano
- 2 cloves of minced garlic
- 1 tbsp of olive oil
- Salt and pepper, to taste

Method of preparation:

1. In a small mixing bowl, combine the lemon juice, oregano, garlic, salt and pepper.
2. Heat a skillet over medium-high heat and add olive oil.
3. Add the pork slices and cook for 2-3 minutes per side or until browned.
4. Remove the pork from skillet and set it aside.
5. Add the lemon juice mixture to the skillet and stir until well combined.
6. Return the pork slices to skillet and toss to coat with the sauce.
7. Cook for an additional 1-2 minutes or until the pork is cooked through.
8. Serve the pork hot and enjoy!

Nutritional facts (per serving): Calories: 260 Fat: 8g | Protein: 34g | Carbohydrates: 2g | Fiber: 0g | Sugar: 1g

STEWS AND SOUP

1. LENTIL AND VEGETABLE SOUP:

A hearty and healthy soup made with lentils, vegetables, and spices, simmered to create a satisfying and nutritious meal.
Prep time: 15 minutes
Cook time: 45 minutes
Serving: 6 people
Yield: 6 servings

Ingredients:
- 1 cup of green lentils, rinsed
- 1 onion, diced
- 2 cloves of garlic, minced
- 2 cups of diced carrots
- 2 cups of diced celery
- 2 cups of diced potatoes
- 4 cups of vegetable broth
- 2 cups of water
- 1 tsp of cumin powder
- 1 tsp of dried thyme
- Salt and pepper, to taste

Method of preparation:
1. In a large pot, sauté the onion and garlic in a little bit of oil until softened.
2. Add the lentils, carrots, celery, potatoes, broth, water, cumin, thyme, salt and pepper.
3. Bring the soup to a boil, then reduce the heat and simmer for 30-40 minutes or until the lentils and vegetables are tender.
4. Serve the soup warm and enjoy!

Nutritional facts (per serving): Calories: 210 | Fat: 1g | Protein: 11g | Carbohydrates: 41g | Fiber: 13g | Sugar: 6g

2. SWEET POTATO AND BLACK BEAN STEW

A hearty and healthy stew made with sweet potatoes, black beans, and spices, simmered to create a satisfying and nutritious meal.
Prep time: 15 minutes
Cook time: 45 minutes
Serving: 6 people
Yield: 6 servings

Ingredients:
- 2 medium sweet potatoes, peeled and diced
- 1 onion, diced
- 2 cloves of garlic, minced
- 2 cups of diced bell pepper
- 2 cups of diced zucchini
- 2 cans of black beans, drained and rinsed
- 4 cups of vegetable broth
- 2 cups of water
- 1 tsp of cumin powder
- 1 tsp of chili powder
- Salt and pepper, to taste

Method of preparation:
1. In a large pot, sauté the onion and garlic in a little bit of oil until softened.
2. Add the sweet potatoes, bell pepper, zucchini, black beans, broth, water, cumin, chili powder, salt and pepper.
3. Bring the stew to a boil, then reduce the heat and simmer for 30-40 minutes or until the vegetables are tender.
4. Serve the stew warm and enjoy!

Nutritional facts (per serving):

Calories: 260 | Fat: 2g | Protein: 11g | Carbohydrates: 52g | Fiber: 12g | Sugar: 8g

3. SPLIT PEA AND HAM SOUP

A hearty and comforting soup made with split peas, ham, and vegetables, simmered to create a satisfying and nutritious meal.
Prep time: 15 minutes
Cook time: 1 hour
Serving: 6 people
Yield: 6 servings

Ingredients:
- 1 cup of split peas, rinsed
- 1 onion, diced
- 2 cloves of garlic, minced
- 2 cups of diced carrots
- 2 cups of diced celery
- 2 cups of diced potatoes
- 4 cups of chicken broth
- 2 cups of water
- 1 lb of diced ham
- 1 tsp of dried thyme
- Salt and pepper, to taste

Method of preparation:
1. In a large pot, sauté the onion and garlic in a little bit of oil until softened.
2. Add the split peas, carrots, celery, potatoes, broth, water, ham, thyme, salt and pepper.
3. Bring the soup to a boil, then reduce the heat and simmer for 45-60 minutes or until the split peas and vegetables are tender.
4. Serve the soup warm and enjoy!

Nutritional facts (per serving):
Calories: 350 | Fat: 10g | Protein: 25g | Carbohydrates: 40g | Fiber: 10g | Sugar: 8g

4. CHICKEN AND VEGETABLE SOUP

A comforting and healthy soup made with chicken, vegetables, and spices, simmered to create a satisfying and nutritious meal.
Prep time: 15 minutes
Cook time: 45 minutes
Serving: 6 people
Yield: 6 servings

Ingredients:
- 2 cups of diced cooked chicken
- 1 onion, diced
- 2 cloves of garlic, minced
- 2 cups of diced carrots
- 2 cups of diced celery
- 2 cups of diced potatoes
- 4 cups of chicken broth
- 2 cups of water
- 1 tsp of dried thyme
- Salt and pepper, to taste

Method of preparation:
1. In a large pot, sauté the onion and garlic in a little bit of oil until softened.
2. Add the chicken, carrots, celery, potatoes, broth, water, thyme, salt and pepper.
3. Bring the soup to a boil, then reduce the heat and simmer for 30-40 minutes or until the vegetables are tender.
4. Serve the soup warm and enjoy!

Nutritional facts (per serving):
Calories: 210 | Fat: 5g | Protein: 18g | Carbohydrates: 22g | Fiber: 3g | Sugar: 6g

5. MOROCCAN CHICKEN STEW

A flavorful and healthy stew made with chicken, vegetables, and spices, simmered to create a satisfying and nutritious meal.
Prep time: 15 minutes
Cook time: 45 minutes
Serving: 6 people
Yield: 6 servings

Ingredients:
- 2 cups of diced cooked chicken
- 1 onion, diced
- 2 cloves of garlic, minced
- 2 cups of diced bell pepper
- 2 cups of diced zucchini
- 1 can of diced tomatoes
- 2 cups of chicken broth
- 2 cups of water
- 1 tsp of cumin powder
- 1 tsp of cinnamon powder
- 1 tsp of paprika powder
- Salt and pepper, to taste

Method of preparation:
1. In a large pot, sauté the onion and garlic in a little bit of oil until softened.
2. Add the chicken, bell pepper, zucchini, tomatoes, broth, water, cumin, cinnamon, paprika, salt and pepper.
3. Bring the stew to a boil, then reduce the heat and simmer for 30-40 minutes or until the vegetables are tender.
4. Serve the stew warm and enjoy!

Nutritional facts (per serving):
Calories: 210 | Fat: 5g | Protein: 18g | Carbohydrates: 22g | Fiber: 3g | Sugar: 6g

6. LENTIL AND KALE SOUP

A hearty and healthy soup made with lentils, kale, and spices, simmered to create a satisfying and nutritious meal.
Prep time: 15 minutes
Cook time: 45 minutes
Serving: 6 people
Yield: 6 servings

Ingredients:
- 1 cup of green lentils, rinsed
- 1 onion, diced
- 2 cloves of garlic, minced
- 2 cups of diced carrots
- 2 cups of diced celery
- 2 cups of diced potatoes
- 4 cups of vegetable broth
- 2 cups of water
- 2 cups of chopped kale
- 1 tsp of cumin powder
- 1 tsp of dried thyme
- Salt and pepper, to taste

Method of preparation:
1. In a large pot, sauté the onion and garlic in a little bit of oil until softened.
2. Add the lentils, carrots, celery, potatoes, broth, water, kale, cumin, thyme, salt and pepper.
3. Bring the soup to a boil, then reduce the heat and simmer for 30-40 minutes or until the lentils and vegetables are tender.
4. Serve the soup warm and enjoy!

Nutritional facts (per serving):
Calories: 210 | Fat: 1g | Protein: 11g | Carbohydrates: 41g | Fiber: 13g | Sugar: 6g

7. BEEF AND VEGETABLE STEW

A hearty and comforting stew made with beef, vegetables, and spices, simmered to create a satisfying and nutritious meal.
Prep time: 15 minutes
Cook time: 1 hour
Serving: 6 people
Yield: 6 servings

Ingredients:
- 1 lb of beef stew meat, cut into small pieces
- 1 onion, diced
- 2 cloves of garlic, minced
- 2 cups of diced carrots
- 2 cups of diced celery
- 2 cups of diced potatoes
- 4 cups of beef broth
- 2 cups of water
- 1 tsp of dried thyme
- Salt and pepper, to taste

Method of preparation:
1. In a large pot, sauté the onion and garlic in a little bit of oil until softened.
2. Add the beef, carrots, celery, potatoes, broth, water, thyme, salt and pepper.
3. Bring the stew to a boil, then reduce the heat and simmer for 45-60 minutes or until the beef and vegetables are tender.
4. Serve the stew warm and enjoy!

Nutritional facts (per serving):
Calories: 310 | Fat: 12g | Protein: 27g | Carbohydrates: 25g | Fiber: 4g | Sugar: 6g

8. TURKEY AND WILD RICE SOUP

A comforting and healthy soup made with turkey, wild rice, and vegetables, simmered to create a satisfying and nutritious meal.
Prep time: 15 minutes
Cook time: 45 minutes
Serving: 6 people
Yield: 6 servings

Ingredients:
- 2 cups of diced cooked turkey
- 1 onion, diced
- 2 cloves of garlic, minced
- 2 cups of diced carrots
- 2 cups of diced celery
- 2 cups of diced potatoes
- 4 cups of chicken broth
- 2 cups of water
- 1 cup of wild rice
- 1 tsp of dried thyme
- Salt and pepper, to taste

Method of preparation:
1. In a large pot, sauté the onion and garlic in a little bit of oil until softened.
2. Add the turkey, carrots, celery, potatoes, broth, water, wild rice, thyme, salt and pepper.
3. Bring the soup to a boil, then reduce the heat and simmer for 30-40 minutes or until the vegetables and rice are tender.
4. Serve the soup warm and enjoy!

Nutritional facts (per serving):
Calories: 310 | Fat: 12g | Protein: 27g | Carbohydrates: 25g | Fiber: 4g | Sugar: 6g

9. CAULIFLOWER AND POTATO SOUP:

A creamy and healthy soup made with cauliflower, potatoes, and spices, simmered to create a satisfying and nutritious meal.
Prep time: 15 minutes
Cook time: 45 minutes
Serving: 6 people
Yield: 6 servings

Ingredients:
- 1 head of cauliflower, chopped
- 2 medium potatoes, peeled and diced
- 1 onion, diced
- 2 cloves of garlic, minced
- 4 cups of vegetable broth
- 2 cups of water
- 1 cup of heavy cream or coconut milk
- 1 tsp of dried thyme
- Salt and pepper, to taste

Method of preparation:
1. In a large pot, sauté the onion and garlic in a little bit of oil until softened.
2. Add the cauliflower, potatoes, broth, water, thyme, salt and pepper.
3. Bring the soup to a boil, then reduce the heat and simmer for 30-40 minutes or until the vegetables are tender.
4. Remove the pot from the heat and use an immersion blender to puree the soup until smooth.
5. Add the cream or coconut milk and stir to combine.
6. Serve the soup warm and enjoy!

Nutritional facts (per serving):
Calories: 210 | Fat: 18g | Protein: 3g | Carbohydrates: 14g | Fiber: 3g | Sugar: 3g

10. VEGETABLE AND CHICKPEA STEW

A flavorful and healthy stew made with vegetables, chickpeas, and spices, simmered to create a satisfying and nutritious meal.
Prep time: 15 minutes
Cook time: 45 minutes
Serving: 6 people
Yield: 6 servings

Ingredients:
- 1 onion, diced
- 2 cloves of garlic, minced
- 2 cups of diced carrots
- 2 cups of diced celery
- 2 cups of diced potatoes
- 2 cups of diced bell pepper
- 2 cans of chickpeas, drained and rinsed
- 4 cups of vegetable broth
- 2 cups of water
- 1 tsp of cumin powder
- 1 tsp of paprika powder
- Salt and pepper, to taste

Method of preparation:
1. In a large pot, sauté the onion and garlic in a little bit of oil until softened.
2. Add the carrots, celery, potatoes, bell pepper, chickpeas, broth, water, cumin, paprika, salt and pepper.
3. Bring the stew to a boil, then reduce the heat and simmer for 30-40 minutes or until the vegetables are tender.
4. Serve the stew warm and enjoy!

Nutritional facts (per serving): Calories: 210 | Fat: 5g | Protein: 11g | Carbohydrates: 31g | Fiber: 9g | Sugar: 6g

11. BUTTERNUT SQUASH AND APPLE SOUP

A creamy and flavorful soup made with butternut squash, apples, and spices, simmered to create a satisfying and nutritious meal.
Prep time: 15 minutes
Cook time: 45 minutes
Serving: 6 people
Yield: 6 servings

Ingredients:
- 1 butternut squash, peeled and diced
- 2 medium apples, peeled and diced
- 1 onion, diced
- 2 cloves of garlic, minced
- 4 cups of vegetable broth
- 2 cups of water
- 1 cup of heavy cream or coconut milk
- 1 tsp of cinnamon powder
- Salt and pepper, to taste

Method of preparation:
1. In a large pot, sauté the onion and garlic in a little bit of oil until softened.
2. Add the butternut squash, apples, broth, water, cinnamon, salt and pepper.
3. Bring the soup to a boil, then reduce the heat and simmer for 30-40 minutes or until the vegetables are tender.
4. Remove the pot from the heat and use an immersion blender to puree the soup until smooth.
5. Add the cream or coconut milk and stir to combine.
6. Serve the soup warm and enjoy!

Nutritional facts (per serving): Calories: 210 | Fat: 18g | Protein: 3g | Carbohydrates: 14g | Fiber: 3g | Sugar: 3g

12. BLACK BEAN AND SWEET POTATO CHILI

A hearty and flavorful chili made with black beans, sweet potatoes, and spices, simmered to create a satisfying and nutritious meal.
Prep time: 15 minutes
Cook time: 45 minutes
Serving: 6 people
Yield: 6 servings

Ingredients:
- 2 cans of black beans, drained and rinsed
- 2 medium sweet potatoes, peeled and diced
- 1 onion, diced
- 2 cloves of garlic, minced
- 2 cups of diced bell pepper
- 2 cups of diced tomatoes
- 4 cups of vegetable broth
- 1 tsp of cumin powder
- 1 tsp of chili powder
- Salt and pepper, to taste

Method of preparation:
1. In a large pot, sauté the onion and garlic in a little bit of oil until softened.
2. Add the black beans, sweet potatoes, bell pepper, tomatoes, broth, cumin, chili powder, salt and pepper.
3. Bring the chili to a boil, then reduce the heat and simmer for 30-40 minutes or until the vegetables are tender.
4. Serve the chili warm and enjoy!

Nutritional facts (per serving):
Calories: 210 | Fat: 5g | Protein: 11g | Carbohydrates: 31g | Fiber: 9g | Sugar: 6g

13. CARROT AND GINGER SOUP

A flavorful and healthy soup made with carrots, ginger, and spices, simmered to create a satisfying and nutritious meal.
Prep time: 15 minutes
Cook time: 45 minutes
Serving: 6 people
Yield: 6 servings

Ingredients:
- 2 cups of diced carrots
- 2 cups of diced onions
- 2 cloves of garlic, minced
- 2 tablespoons of freshly grated ginger
- 4 cups of vegetable broth
- 2 cups of water
- 1 tsp of cumin powder
- Salt and pepper, to taste

Method of preparation:
1. In a large pot, sauté the onions and garlic in a little bit of oil until softened.
2. Add the carrots, ginger, broth, water, cumin, salt and pepper.
3. Bring the soup to a boil, then reduce the heat and simmer for 30-40 minutes or until the vegetables are tender.
4. Remove the pot from the heat and use an immersion blender to puree the soup until smooth.
5. Serve the soup warm and enjoy!

Nutritional facts (per serving):
Calories: 120 | Fat: 2g | Protein: 3g | Carbohydrates: 23g | Fiber: 5g | Sugar: 10g

14. MINESTRONE SOUP

A classic and hearty soup made with a variety of vegetables, beans, and pasta, simmered to create a satisfying and nutritious meal.

Prep time: 15 minutes
Cook time: 45 minutes
Serving: 6 people
Yield: 6 servings

Ingredients:
- 1 onion, diced
- 2 cloves of garlic, minced
- 2 cups of diced carrots
- 2 cups of diced celery
- 2 cups of diced zucchini
- 2 cups of diced potatoes
- 2 cups of diced tomatoes
- 2 cans of cannellini beans, drained and rinsed
- 4 cups of vegetable broth
- 2 cups of water
- 1 cup of small pasta, such as ditalini or elbow macaroni
- 1 tsp of dried thyme
- Salt and pepper, to taste

Method of preparation:
1. In a large pot, sauté the onion and garlic in a little bit of oil until softened.
2. Add the carrots, celery, zucchini, potatoes, tomatoes, cannellini beans, broth, water, thyme, salt and pepper.
3. Bring the soup to a boil, then reduce the heat and simmer for 30-40 minutes or until the vegetables are tender.
4. Add the pasta and continue to simmer for an additional 10-15 minutes or until the pasta is cooked through.
5. Serve the soup warm and enjoy!

Nutritional facts (per serving):
Calories: 210 | Fat: 5g | Protein: 11g |
Carbohydrates: 31g | Fiber: 9g | Sugar: 6g

15. CHICKEN AND SWEET POTATO STEW

A comforting and healthy stew made with chicken, sweet potatoes, and vegetables, simmered to create a satisfying and nutritious meal.

Prep time: 15 minutes
Cook time: 45 minutes
Serving: 6 people
Yield: 6 servings

Ingredients:
- 1 lb of boneless and skinless chicken breast, diced
- 2 medium sweet potatoes, peeled and diced
- 1 onion, diced
- 2 cloves of garlic, minced
- 2 cups of diced carrots
- 2 cups of diced celery
- 4 cups of chicken broth
- 2 cups of water
- 1 tsp of dried thyme
- Salt and pepper, to taste

Method of preparation:
1. In a large pot, sauté the onion and garlic in a little bit of oil until softened.
2. Add the chicken, sweet potatoes, carrots, celery, broth, water, thyme, salt and pepper.
3. Bring the stew to a boil, then reduce the heat and simmer for 45-60 minutes or until the chicken and vegetables are tender.
4. Serve the stew warm and enjoy!

Nutritional facts (per serving): Calories: 210 | Fat: 5g | Protein: 15g | Carbohydrates: 25g | Fiber: 5g | Sugar: 5g.

SNACKS

1. APPLE SLICES WITH ALMOND BUTTER

This is a simple and healthy snack that combines the sweetness of apple slices with the creamy texture of almond butter.
Prep Time: 5 minutes
Cook Time: None
Serving: 1
Yield: 1 serving

Ingredients:
- 1 apple, thinly sliced
- 2 tablespoons almond butter

Method of preparation:
1. Slice the apple into thin slices.
2. Spread the almond butter over the apple slices.
3. Serve and enjoy!

Nutritional facts (per serving): Calories: 250 | Fat: 18g| Sodium: 0mg | Carbohydrates: 25g | Fiber: 5g | Protein: 6g.

2. BERRY SMOOTHIE WITH CHIA SEEDS

This smoothie is a delicious and healthy way to start your day. The combination of berries and chia seeds provides a powerful boost of antioxidants and omega-3 fatty acids.
Prep Time: 5 minutes
Cook Time: None
Serving: 1
Yield: 1 serving

Ingredients:

- 1 cup frozen berries (strawberries, blueberries, raspberries)
- 1 banana
- 1/2 cup Greek yogurt
- 1/2 cup almond milk
- 1 tablespoon chia seeds

Method of preparation:
1. Add the berries, banana, Greek yogurt, and almond milk to a blender.
2. Blend until smooth.
3. Stir in the chia seeds.
4. Pour into a glass and enjoy!

Nutritional facts (per serving)
Calories: 250 | Fat: 8g | Sodium: 40mgCarbohydrates: 40g | Fiber: 10g | Protein: 12g

3. CARROTS AND HUMMUS

This is a simple and healthy snack that combines the crunch of carrots with the creaminess of hummus.
Prep Time: 5 minutes
Cook Time: None
Serving: 1
Yield: 1 serving

Ingredients:

- 2 carrots, peeled and cut into sticks
- 2 tablespoons hummus

Method of preparation:
1. Wash and cut the carrots into sticks.
2. Serve the hummus on a plate or bowl.
3. Dip the carrot sticks in the hummus.
4. Enjoy!

Nutritional facts (per serving):| Calories: 70 | Fat: 4g | Sodium: 80mg | Carbohydrates: 8gFiber: 2g | Protein: 2g

4. CUCUMBER SLICES WITH TZATZIKI SAUCE

This is a refreshing and healthy snack that combines the crispness of cucumber slices with the tangy flavor of tzatziki sauce.
Prep Time: 10 minutes
Cook Time: None
Serving: 1
Yield: 1 serving

Ingredients:

- 1 cucumber, thinly sliced
- 1/4 cup tzatziki sauce

Method of preparation:
1. Slice the cucumber into thin slices.
2. Serve the tzatziki sauce on a plate or bowl.
3. Dip the cucumber slices in the tzatziki sauce.
4. Enjoy!

Nutritional facts (per serving):
Calories: 50 | Fat: 3g| Sodium: 110mg| Carbohydrates: 5g| Fiber: 1g| Protein: 2g

5. DEVILED EGGS WITH AVOCADO

This is a healthy twist on a classic deviled egg recipe. The avocado adds a creamy texture and a boost of healthy fats.
Prep Time: 10 minutes
Cook Time: 10 minutes
Serving: 1
Yield: 2 deviled eggs

Ingredients:

- 2 eggs
- 1 avocado
- 1 teaspoon Dijon mustard

- 1 teaspoon mayonnaise
- Salt and pepper, to taste

Method of preparation:
1. Place the eggs in a saucepan and cover with water. Bring to a boil, then reduce the heat and simmer for 10 minutes.
2. Remove the eggs from the water and place in a bowl of ice water to cool.
3. Peel the eggs and slice them in half lengthwise.
4. Remove the yolks and place them in a separate bowl.
5. Mash the avocado and add it to the yolks along with the mustard, mayonnaise, salt, and pepper. Mix well.
6. Spoon the mixture into the egg whites.
7. Serve and enjoy!

Nutritional facts (per serving): Calories: 250 | Fat: 22g| Sodium: 130mg|
Carbohydrates: 6g| Fiber: 3g| Protein: 8g

.6. EDAMAME WITH SEA SALT

This is a simple and healthy snack that combines the protein-rich soybeans with the flavor of sea salt.
Prep Time: 5 minutes
Cook Time: 5 minutes
Serving: 1
Yield: 1 serving

Ingredients:
- 1 cup of edamame (fresh or frozen)
- 1 teaspoon sea salt

Method of preparation:
1. Bring a pot of water to a boil.
2. Add the edamame and cook for 5 minutes.
3. Drain the edamame and place them in a bowl.
4. Sprinkle sea salt on top and toss to coat.
5. Serve and enjoy!

Nutritional facts (per serving): Calories: 150 | Fat: 8g | Sodium: 580mg |
Carbohydrates: 9g | Fiber: 5g | Protein: 11g

7. GREEK YOGURT WITH BERRIES AND HONEY

This is a delicious and healthy snack that combines the protein-rich Greek yogurt with the sweetness of berries and honey.
Prep Time: 5 minutes
Cook Time: None
Serving: 1
Yield: 1 serving

Ingredients:
- 1 cup Greek yogurt
- 1/2 cup mixed berries
- 1 tablespoon honey

Method of preparation:
1. In a bowl, combine Greek yogurt, mixed berries and honey.
2. Mix them well.
3. Enjoy!

Nutritional facts (per serving):
Calories: 250 | Fat: 5g | Sodium: 75mg |
Carbohydrates: 35g| Fiber: 2g| Protein: 20g

8. GRILLED EGGPLANT WITH TAHINI AND LEMON

This is a healthy and flavorful snack that combines the smoky flavor of grilled eggplant with the tangy flavor of tahini and lemon.

Prep Time: 10 minutes
Cook Time: 10 minutes
Serving: 1
Yield: 1 serving

Ingredients:

- 1 eggplant, sliced
- 2 tablespoons tahini
- 1 tablespoon lemon juice
- 1 clove garlic, minced
- Salt and pepper, to taste

Method of preparation:

1. Preheat a grill to medium-high heat.
2. Season the eggplant slices with salt and pepper.
3. Grill the eggplant slices for 5 minutes per side, or until tender.
4. In a small bowl, mix together the tahini, lemon juice, garlic, salt, and pepper.
5. Serve the grilled eggplant with the tahini mixture on top.
6. Enjoy!

Nutritional facts (per serving):
Calories: 200 | Fat: 15g| Sodium: 120mg|
Carbohydrates: 15g | Fiber: 7g | Protein: 5g

9. GUACAMOLE WITH VEGGIES

This is a healthy and delicious snack that combines the creaminess of guacamole with the crunch of fresh veggies.
Prep Time: 10 minutes
Cook Time: None
Serving: 1
Yield: 1 serving

Ingredients:

- 1 avocado, mashed
- 1 tablespoon lime juice
- 1 clove garlic, minced
- Salt and pepper, to taste
- 1/4 cup diced tomatoes
- 1/4 cup diced cucumber
- 1/4 cup diced bell pepper
- Veggies of your choice for dipping (carrots, celery, bell pepper, etc)

Method of preparation:

1. In a medium bowl, mash the avocado with a fork or a potato masher.
2. Stir in the lime juice, garlic, salt, and pepper.
3. Mix in the diced tomatoes, cucumber, and bell pepper.
4. Serve with veggies of your choice for dipping.
5. Enjoy!

Nutritional facts (per serving): Calories: 150 | Fat: 13g| Sodium: 10mg|Carbohydrates: 9g| Fiber: 6g| Protein: 2g

10. KALE CHIPS WITH OLIVE OIL AND SEA SALT

This is a healthy and crispy snack that combines the nutrient-rich kale with the flavor of olive oil and sea salt.
Prep Time: 10 minutes
Cook Time: 15 minutes
Serving: 1
Yield: 1 serving

Ingredients:

- 1 bunch of kale, washed and dried
- 1 tablespoon olive oil
- 1 teaspoon sea salt

Method of preparation:

1. Preheat the oven to 350 degrees F.

2. Remove the kale leaves from the thick stems and tear them into bite-size pieces.
3. In a large bowl, toss the kale with the olive oil and sea salt.
4. Spread the kale onto a baking sheet in a single layer.
5. Bake for 15 minutes, or until the edges are brown and crispy.
6. Enjoy!

Nutritional facts (per serving): Calories: 70 | Fat: 6g | Sodium: 480mg | Carbohydrates: 5g | Fiber: 1g | Protein: 2g

11. LENTIL DIP WITH VEGGIES

This is a healthy and flavorful snack that combines the protein-rich lentils with the crunch of fresh veggies.
Prep Time: 10 minutes
Cook Time: 20 minutes
Serving: 1
Yield: 1 serving

Ingredients:
- 1/2 cup cooked lentils
- 1 tablespoon olive oil
- 1 tablespoon lemon juice
- 1 clove garlic, minced
- Salt and pepper, to taste
- Veggies of your choice for dipping (carrots, celery, bell pepper, etc)

Method of preparation:
1. In a food processor, blend the cooked lentils, olive oil, lemon juice, garlic, salt, and pepper until smooth.
2. Serve with veggies of your choice for dipping.
3. Enjoy!

Nutritional facts (per serving): Calories: 150 | Fat: 8g| Sodium: 40mg | Carbohydrates: 16g | Fiber: 7g | Protein: 7g

12. Mixed Nuts With Dried Fruit

This is a healthy and satisfying snack that combines the protein and healthy fats of mixed nuts with the natural sweetness of dried fruit.
Prep Time: 5 minutes
Cook Time: None
Serving: 1
Yield: 1 serving

Ingredients:
- 1/4 cup mixed nuts (almonds, walnuts, cashews, etc)
- 1/4 cup dried fruit (raisins, cranberries, apricots, etc)

Method of preparation:
1. In a small bowl, combine the mixed nuts and dried fruit.
2. Mix well.
3. Enjoy!

Nutritional facts (per serving): Calories: 250 | Fat: 20g | Sodium: 10mg| Carbohydrates: 20g | Fiber: 3g | Protein: 6g

13. OAT AND SEED BARS WITH HONEY

This is a healthy and satisfying snack that combines the nutrition of oats and seeds with the natural sweetness of honey.
Prep Time: 10 minutes
Cook Time: 25 minutes
Serving: 1

Yield: 8 bars
INGREDIENTS:
- 1 cup rolled oats
- 1/2 cup mixed seeds (sunflower seeds, pumpkin seeds, flaxseeds, etc)
- 1/4 cup honey
- 1/4 cup almond butter

Method of preparation:
1. Preheat the oven to 350 degrees F.
2. In a medium bowl, combine the oats and seeds.
3. In a small saucepan, heat the honey and almond butter over low heat until melted.
4. Pour the honey mixture over the oat mixture and stir until well combined.
5. Press the mixture into a greased 8x8 inch baking dish.
6. Bake for 25 minutes or until golden brown.
7. Let cool and cut into bars.
8. Enjoy!

Nutritional facts (per serving): |
Calories: 200 | Fat: 12g | Sodium: 10mg | Carbohydrates: 20g | Fiber: 3g | Protein: 6g

14. POPCORN WITH NUTRITIONAL YEAST AND SEA SALT

This is a healthy and tasty snack that combines the crunch of popcorn with the cheesy flavor of nutritional yeast and sea salt.
Prep Time: 5 minutes
Cook Time: 5 minutes
Serving: 1

Yield: 1 serving
Ingredients:
- 1/2 cup popcorn kernels
- 2 tablespoons nutritional yeast
- 1 teaspoon sea salt

Method of preparation:
1. Heat a large pot with a tight-fitting lid over medium-high heat.
2. Add the popcorn kernels and cover the pot.
3. Shake the pot occasionally until the popping slows down.
4. Popcorn with Nutritional Yeast and Sea Salt (Continued)
5. Once the popping slows down, remove the pot from the heat.
6. In a small bowl, mix together the nutritional yeast and sea salt.
7. Sprinkle the mixture over the popcorn and toss to coat.
8. Enjoy!

NUTRITIONAL FACTS (per serving):
Calories: 100 | Fat: 2g | Sodium: 480mg | | Carbohydrates: 18g | Fiber: 3g | Protein: 5g

15. QUINOA CRACKERS WITH HUMMUS

This is a healthy and satisfying snack that combines the protein-rich quinoa crackers with the creaminess of hummus.
Prep Time: 10 minutes
Cook Time: 15 minutes
Serving: 1
Yield: 20 crackers
Ingredients:
1/2 cup quinoa flour
1/4 cup flaxseed meal
1/4 cup water

1/4 teaspoon sea salt

1/4 cup hummus

Method of preparation:

1. Preheat the oven to 350 degrees F.
2. In a medium bowl, mix together the quinoa flour, flaxseed meal, water, and sea salt.
3. Roll out the dough between two sheets of parchment paper to 1/8-inch thickness.
4. Use a knife or pizza cutter to cut the dough into cracker-size shapes.
5. Place the crackers on a baking sheet and bake for 15 minutes or until golden brown.
6. Serve the crackers with hummus on the side.

NUTRITIONAL FACTS (per serving):

Calories: 50 | Fat: 2g | Sodium: 70mg | Carbohydrates: 6g | Fiber: 1g | Protein: 2g

DESSERT

1. BERRIES WITH BALSAMIC GLAZE:

A simple yet delicious brunch dish made with fresh berries drizzled with a sweet and tangy balsamic glaze.

Prep time: 5 minutes
Cook time: 10 minutes
Serving: 4 people
Yield: 4 servings

Ingredients:

- 2 cups of mixed berries (such as strawberries, raspberries, blackberries, and blueberries)
- 1/4 cup of balsamic vinegar
- 2 tbsp of honey
- 1 tsp of cornstarch
- 1 tsp of water

Method of preparation:

1. In a small saucepan, combine the balsamic vinegar and honey. Bring to a simmer over medium heat.
2. In a small bowl, mix the cornstarch and water together to create a slurry.
3. Slowly pour the slurry into the saucepan with the balsamic and honey mixture, stirring constantly.
4. Cook for an additional 2-3 minutes, or until the mixture thickens.
5. Remove from heat and let it cool for a few minutes.
6. Place the berries in a serving dish, and pour the balsamic glaze over the berries.
7. Serve and enjoy!

Nutritional facts (per serving): Calories: 70 | Fat: 0g | Protein: 1g | Carbohydrates: 18g | Fiber: 2g | Sugar: 14g

2. BLUEBERRY SORBET

A refreshing and healthy brunch dish made with fresh blueberries and a touch of honey, frozen and blended to create a delicious sorbet.

Prep time: 10 minutes
Cook time: 0 minutes
Serving: 4 people
Yield: 4 servings

Ingredients:

- 2 cups of fresh blueberries
- 1/4 cup of honey
- 1/4 cup of water
- squeeze of lemon juice

Method of preparation:

1. In a blender, combine the blueberries, honey, water, and lemon juice. Blend until smooth.
2. Pour the mixture into a loaf pan and freeze for at least 4 hours or until firm.
3. Scoop the sorbet into individual serving dishes and serve immediately.

Nutritional facts (per serving): Calories: 80 | Fat: 0g| Protein: 1g| Carbohydrates: 21g| Fiber: 2g| Sugar: 17g

3. CHOCOLATE AVOCADO MOUSSE

A rich and creamy brunch dish made with ripe avocados, cocoa powder and honey, blended to create a delicious and healthy chocolate mousse.

Prep time: 10 minutes
Cook time: 0 minutes
Serving: 4 people
Yield: 4 servings

Ingredients:

2 ripe avocados
1/4 cup of cocoa powder
2 tbsp of honey
1 tsp of vanilla extract
pinch of salt

Method of preparation

8. Cut the avocados in half and remove the pit. Scoop out the flesh and place it in a food processor or blender.
9. Add the cocoa powder, honey, vanilla extract, and salt to the food processor.
10. Blend until smooth and creamy.
11. Taste and adjust sweetness and seasoning as needed.
12. Spoon the mousse into individual serving dishes and chill in the refrigerator for at least 30 minutes before serving.

Nutritional facts (per serving):
Calories: 150 | Fat: 12g | Protein: 2g | Carbohydrates: 12g | Fiber: 6g | Sugar: 7g

4. COCONUT MILK ICE CREAM

A creamy and delicious brunch dish made with coconut milk, honey and vanilla extract, frozen and blended to create a healthy and dairy-free ice cream.

Prep time: 10 minutes
Cook time: 0 minutes
Serving: 4 people
Yield: 4 servings

Ingredients:

1 can of full-fat coconut milk
1/4 cup of honey
1 tsp of vanilla extract
pinch of salt

Method of preparation:

1. In a medium mixing bowl, whisk together the coconut milk, honey, vanilla extract, and salt until well combined.
2. Pour the mixture into a loaf pan and freeze for at least 4 hours or until firm.
3. Scoop the ice cream into individual serving dishes and serve immediately.

Nutritional facts (per serving):
Calories: 200 | Fat: 18g | Protein: 1g| Carbohydrates: 14g| Fiber: 0g| Sugar: 12g

5. DARK CHOCOLATE BARK WITH NUTS AND SEEDS

A healthy and delicious brunch dish made with dark chocolate, mixed nuts and seeds, and a touch of sea salt, for a satisfying and nutritious treat.
Prep time: 10 minutes
Cook time: 0 minutes
Serving: 4 people
Yield: 4 servings

Ingredients:
- 8 oz of dark chocolate
- 1/4 cup of mixed nuts (such as almonds, walnuts, and pistachios)
- 1/4 cup of mixed seeds (such as pumpkin, sunflower and sesame)
- pinch of sea salt

Method of preparation:
1. Line a baking sheet with parchment paper.
2. Melt the chocolate in a double boiler or in the microwave.
3. Spread the melted chocolate onto the prepared baking sheet.

4. Sprinkle the mixed nuts, mixed seeds and sea salt on top of the chocolate.
5. Chill in the refrigerator for at least 30 minutes until set.
6. Break the chocolate bark into pieces and enjoy!

Nutritional facts (per serving):
Calories: 260 | Fat: 22g | Protein: 4g | Carbohydrates: 16g | Fiber: 3g | Sugar: 12g

6. FRESH FRUIT SALAD

A refreshing and healthy brunch dish made with a variety of fresh fruits, cut and mixed together for a delicious and nutritious treat.
Prep time: 10 minutes
Cook time: 0 minutes
Serving: 4 people
Yield: 4 servings

Ingredients
- 2 cups of mixed fresh fruits (such as berries, melons, kiwi, and pineapple)
- 1 tbsp of honey
- 1 tbsp of lime juice
- 1 tsp of mint leaves, chopped

Method of preparation:
1. Cut the fruits into bite-sized pieces and place them in a large mixing bowl.
2. In a small mixing bowl, combine the honey, lime juice, and mint leaves.
3. Pour the dressing over the fruit and toss gently to coat.
4. Divide the fruit salad into individual serving dishes and enjoy!

Nutritional facts (per serving): Calories: 100 | Fat: 0.5g| Protein: 1g | Carbohydrates: 26g | Fiber: 3g | Sugar: 20g

7. GRILLED PEACHES WITH HONEY

A simple yet delicious brunch dish made with fresh peaches, grilled and drizzled with honey for added sweetness.

Prep time: 5 minutes
Cook time: 10 minutes
Serving: 4 people
Yield: 4 servings

Ingredients:
- 4 ripe peaches
- 2 tbsp of honey

Method of preparation:
1. Preheat the grill to medium-high heat.
2. Cut the peaches in half and remove the pit.
3. Place the peaches on the grill, cut side down. Grill for 5-7 minutes, or until the peaches are slightly softened and have grill marks.
4. Remove the peaches from the grill and drizzle with honey.
5. Serve the peaches hot and enjoy!

Nutritional facts (per serving): Calories: 90 | Fat: 0g | Protein: 1g | Carbohydrates: 24g | Fiber: 2g| Sugar: 21g

8. LEMON BARS WITH ALMOND CRUST

A delicious and tangy brunch dish made with a buttery almond crust and a lemon curd filling.

Prep time: 15 minutes
Cook time: 45 minutes
Serving: 9 people
Yield: 9 servings

Ingredients:
- 1 cup of almond flour
- 1/4 cup of butter, melted
- 2 tbsp of honey
- 3 eggs
- 1/2 cup of lemon juice
- 1/2 cup of honey
- 1/4 cup of flour
- Powdered sugar, for dusting

Method of preparation:
1. Preheat the oven to 350 degrees F (175 degrees C). Grease a 9x9 inch baking pan.
2. In a medium mixing bowl, combine the almond flour, melted butter, and 2 tablespoons of honey. Press the mixture into the bottom of the prepared baking pan.
3. Bake the crust for 10-12 minutes, or until golden brown.
4. In a separate mixing bowl, whisk together the eggs, lemon juice, 1/2 cup of honey, and flour. Pour the mixture over the crust.
5. Bake for an additional 20-25 minutes, or until the filling is set.
6. Let the bars cool completely, then dust with powdered sugar before cutting and serving.

Nutritional facts (per serving):
Calories: 210 | Fat: 15g | Protein: 5g | Carbohydrates: 16g | Fiber: 1g | Sugar: 11g

9. MANGO LASSI

A delicious and refreshing brunch dish made with ripe mangoes, yogurt, and honey, blended together to create a creamy and nutritious smoothie.

Prep time: 10 minutes
Cook time: 0 minutes
Serving: 4 people
Yield: 4 servings

Ingredients:

- 2 ripe mangoes
- 1 cup of plain yogurt
- 1/4 cup of honey
- 1 tsp of cardamom powder
- 2 cups of ice

Method of preparation:

1. Peel and chop the mangoes and place them in a blender.
2. Add the yogurt, honey, cardamom powder and ice.
3. Blend until smooth and creamy.
4. Taste and adjust sweetness as needed.
5. Pour the lassi into individual serving glasses and enjoy immediately.

Nutritional facts (per serving): Calories: 170 | Fat: 1g | Protein: 5g | Carbohydrates: 39g | Fiber: 2g | Sugar: 32g

10. MIXED BERRY SORBET

A refreshing and healthy brunch dish made with mixed berries, honey, and lime juice, frozen and blended to create a delicious sorbet.
Prep time: 10 minutes
Cook time: 0 minutes
Serving: 4 people
Yield: 4 servings

Ingredients:

- 2 cups of mixed berries (such as strawberries, raspberries, blackberries, and blueberries)
- 1/4 cup of honey
- 1 tbsp of lime juice
- 2 cups of ice

Method of preparation:

1. In a blender, combine the mixed berries, honey, lime juice and ice. Blend until smooth.
2. Pour the mixture into a loaf pan and freeze for at least 4 hours or until firm.
3. Scoop the sorbet into individual serving dishes and serve immediately.

Nutritional facts (per serving): Calories: 80 | Fat: 0g | Protein: 1g | Carbohydrates: 21g | Fiber: 2g | Sugar: 17g

11. OAT AND FRUIT BARS

A healthy and delicious brunch dish made with oats, mixed nuts, mixed dried fruits, and honey, baked to create a satisfying and nutritious bar.
Prep time: 15 minutes
Cook time: 25 minutes
Serving: 16 people
Yield: 16 servings

Ingredients:

- 2 cups of rolled oats
- 1/2 cup of mixed nuts (such as almonds, walnuts, and pecans)
- 1/2 cup of mixed dried fruits (such as cranberries, raisins, and apricots)
- 1/2 cup of honey
- 1/4 cup of coconut oil
- 1 tsp of vanilla extract

Method of preparation:

1. Preheat the oven to 350 degrees F (175 degrees C). Line a 9x9 inch baking pan with parchment paper.

2. In a large mixing bowl, combine the rolled oats, mixed nuts, mixed dried fruits, honey, coconut oil, and vanilla extract. Mix until well combined.
3. Press the mixture into the prepared baking pan.
4. Bake for 20-25 minutes, or until golden brown.
5. Let the bars cool completely before cutting into 16 bars.
6. Serve and enjoy!

Nutritional facts (per serving):
Calories: 200 | Fat: 12g | Protein: 3g | Carbohydrates: 23g | Fiber: 2g | Sugar: 14g

12. PAPAYA BOATS WITH LIME AND MINT

A refreshing and healthy brunch dish made with ripe papayas, filled with a mixture of lime juice, honey and mint leaves, for a delicious and nutritious treat.
Prep time: 10 minutes
Cook time: 0 minutes
Serving: 4 people
Yield: 4 servings

Ingredients:
- 2 ripe papayas
- 2 limes, juiced
- 2 tbsp of honey
- 1 tbsp of mint leaves, chopped

Method of preparation:
1. Cut the papayas in half and remove the seeds.
2. In a small mixing bowl, combine the lime juice, honey, and mint leaves.
3. Spoon the mixture into the papaya halves.

4. Serve the papaya boats chilled and enjoy!

Nutritional facts (per serving):
Calories: 90 | Fat: 0g | Protein: 1g | Carbohydrates: 24g | Fiber: 4g | Sugar: 18g

13. QUINOA PUDDING WITH CINNAMON AND HONEY

A delicious and nutritious brunch dish made with cooked quinoa, milk, honey, and cinnamon, for a satisfying and healthy treat.
Prep time: 5 minutes
Cook time: 20 minutes
Serving: 4 people
Yield: 4 servings

Ingredients:
- 1 cup of cooked quinoa
- 2 cups of milk
- 1/4 cup of honey
- 1 tsp of cinnamon
- pinch of salt

Method of preparation:
1. In a medium saucepan, combine the cooked quinoa, milk, honey, cinnamon, and salt.
2. Bring the mixture to a simmer over medium heat.
3. Reduce the heat to low and continue cooking for 15-20 minutes, or until the quinoa is tender and the mixture has thickened.
4. Taste and adjust sweetness as needed.
5. Divide the pudding into individual serving dishes and chill in the refrigerator for at least 30 minutes before serving.

Nutritional facts (per serving):
Calories: 160 | Fat: 3g | Protein: 6g |
Carbohydrates: 28g | Fiber: 2g | Sugar: 18g

14. ROASTED PLUMS WITH VANILLA AND CINNAMON

A simple yet delicious brunch dish made with fresh plums, roasted with vanilla and cinnamon, for a sweet and healthy treat.
Prep time: 5 minutes
Cook time: 20 minutes
Serving: 4 people
Yield: 4 servings

Ingredients:
- 4 ripe plums
- 1 tsp of vanilla extract
- 1 tsp of cinnamon
- 2 tbsp of honey

Method of preparation:
1. Preheat the oven to 400 degrees F (200 degrees C).
2. Cut the plums in half and remove the pit.
3. In a small mixing bowl, combine the vanilla extract, cinnamon and honey.
4. Place the plums on a baking sheet, cut side up.
5. Brush the plum halves with the mixture.
6. Roast for 20-25 minutes, or until the plums are tender and the mixture is caramelized.
7. Serve the roasted plums warm and enjoy!

Nutritional facts (per serving):
Calories: 80 | Fat: 0g | Protein: 1g |
Carbohydrates: 21g | Fiber: 2g | Sugar: 17g

15. STRAWBERRY SORBET

A refreshing and healthy brunch dish made with fresh strawberries, honey and lime juice, frozen and blended to create a delicious sorbet.
Prep time: 10 minutes
Cook time: 0 minutes
Serving: 4 people
Yield: 4 servings

Ingredients:
2 cups of fresh strawberries
1/4 cup of honey
1 tbsp of lime juice
2 cups of ice

Method of preparation:
1. In a blender, combine the strawberries, honey, lime juice and ice. Blend until smooth.
2. Pour the mixture into a loaf pan and freeze for at least 4 hours or until firm.
3. Scoop the sorbet into individual serving dishes and serve immediately.

Nutritional facts (per serving): Calories: 80 | Fat: 0g | Protein: 1g | Carbohydrates: 21g | Fiber: 2g| Sugar: 17g

Conclusions

Ultimately, the only way to limit the progress of silent inflammation is a lifestyle that incorporates a varied diet that favors natural and vegetable foods rich in fiber, vitamins, and minerals, enriched with beneficial spices, and integrated with the right probiotics.

On the other hand, sugars, refined foods with a high glycemic index, saturated hydrogenated and animal fats, dairy products, and acidifying foods, in general, should be reduced. (remember that the blood pH of a healthy body is about 7.4, i.e., slightly alkaline). Consequently, we will be able to prevent a hyperinsulinemia increase, a condition which keeps the inflammatory state of the body high (it is difficult to detect a disease that does not have some connection with insulin); we will contrast that acidic biological terrain which is a source of illness and psychophysical malaise (cancer cells do not develop in an alkaline environment).

A healthy lifestyle requires more time to be devoted to regular physical activity (even daily) and to the control of cortisol generated by stressful lifestyles and lack of adequate rest.

Recent studies have demonstrated that a diet and a balanced lifestyle can improve aspects of our health because, contrary to what has always been thought, the genetic predisposition to a certain disease does not inexorably define our destiny. In fact, the plasticity of our DNA makes it a structure in continuous adaptation to the stimuli to which we expose our body.

Learning to eat is the only kind of drug that can save us from disease!

30-Day Meal Plan

Day	Breakfast	Lunch	Dinner	Desserts
1	OVERNIGHT OATS WITH CHIA SEEDS, BERRIES, AND ALMOND MILK	LENTIL AND VEGETABLE SOUP	SALMON AND VEGETABLE	BERRIES WITH BALSAMIC GLAZE
2	GREEN SMOOTHIE WITH SPINACH, KALE, AVOCADO, AND GINGER	MINESTRONE SOUP	WHITE BEAN AND KALE SOUP	BLUEBERRY SORBET
3	TURMERIC LATTE WITH ALMOND MILK AND HONEY	TURKEY AND WILD RICE SOUP	Turkey and Vegetable Teriyaki Stir-Fry	CHOCOLATE AVOCADO MOUSSE
4	QUINOA BOWL WITH VEGGIES, AVOCADO, AND A POACHED EGG	BLACK BEAN AND QUINOA SALAD WITH LIME VINAIGRETTE	LENTIL AND VEGETABLE SOUP	COCONUT MILK ICE CREAM
5	SWEET POTATO TOAST WITH ALMOND BUTTER, BANANA, AND CINNAMON	LENTIL AND SWEET POTATO CURRY	ROASTED PORK LOIN WITH GARLIC AND ROSEMARY	DARK CHOCOLATE BARK WITH NUTS AND SEEDS
6	CHIA SEED PUDDING WITH BERRIES AND COCONUT MILK	BLACK BEAN AND VEGETABLE ENCHILADAS	MOROCCAN CHICKEN STEW	FRESH FRUIT SALAD
7	WHOLE GRAIN PANCAKES WITH BLUEBERRIES AND FLAXSEED	WHITE BEAN AND KALE SOUP	BEEF AND VEGETABLE STEW	GRILLED PEACHES WITH HONEY
8	EGG SCRAMBLE WITH BELL PEPPERS, TOMATOES, AND SPINACH	RED LENTIL AND VEGETABLE SOUP	GRILLED BEEF SKEWERS WITH VEGETABLES	LEMON BARS WITH ALMOND CRUST
9	OMELET WITH MUSHROOMS, ONIONS, AND FETA CHEESE	CHICKPEA AND SPINACH CURRY	BEEF AND VEGETABLE STEW	MANGO LASSI
10	YOGURT BOWL WITH BERRIES, NUTS, AND SEEDS	WHOLE GRAIN AND BEAN CHILI	CARROT AND GINGER SOUP	MIXED BERRY SORBET
11	SMOOTHIE BOWL WITH SPINACH, BANANA, AND CHIA SEEDS	BLACK BEAN AND SWEET POTATO ENCHILADAS	WHITE BEAN AND KALE SOUP	OAT AND FRUIT BARS
12	BREAKFAST BURRITO WITH SWEET POTATOES, BLACK BEANS, AND AVOCADO	SALMON AND VEGETABLE TERIYAKI STIR-FRY	TURKEY AND VEGETABLE TERIYAKI STIR-FRY	PAPAYA BOATS WITH LIME AND MINT
13	AVOCADO TOAST WITH POACHED EGG AND SMOKED SALMON	BAKED HALIBUT WITH LEMON AND CAPERS	CUCUMBER SLICES WITH TZATZIKI SAUCE	QUINOA PUDDING WITH CINNAMON AND HONEY
14	BREAKFAST FRITTATA WITH VEGGIES AND FETA CHEESE	BAKED TILAPIA WITH TOMATO AND OLIVE RELISH	ROASTED PORK LOIN WITH GARLIC AND ROSEMARY	ROASTED PLUMS WITH VANILLA AND CINNAMON
15	BREAKFAST HASH WITH SWEET POTATOES, BELL PEPPERS, AND EGGS	PAN-SEARED TILAPIA WITH TOMATOES AND OLIVES	MOROCCAN CHICKEN STEW	STRAWBERRY SORBET
16	OVERNIGHT OATS WITH CHIA SEEDS, BERRIES, AND ALMOND MILK	CHICKPEA AND SPINACH CURRY	CARROT AND GINGER SOUP	BERRIES WITH BALSAMIC GLAZE
17	GREEN SMOOTHIE WITH SPINACH, KALE, AVOCADO, AND GINGER	WHOLE GRAIN AND BEAN CHILI	WHITE BEAN AND KALE SOUP	BLUEBERRY SORBET
18	TURMERIC LATTE WITH ALMOND MILK AND HONEY	BLACK BEAN AND SWEET POTATO ENCHILADAS	TURKEY AND VEGETABLE TERIYAKI STIR-FRY	CHOCOLATE AVOCADO MOUSSE

19	QUINOA BOWL WITH VEGGIES, AVOCADO, AND A POACHED EGG	SALMON AND VEGETABLE TERIYAKI STIR-FRY	LENTIL AND VEGETABLE SOUP	COCONUT MILK ICE CREAM
20	SWEET POTATO TOAST WITH ALMOND BUTTER, BANANA, AND CINNAMON	BAKED HALIBUT WITH LEMON AND CAPERS	ROASTED PORK LOIN WITH GARLIC AND ROSEMARY	DARK CHOCOLATE BARK WITH NUTS AND SEEDS
21	CHIA SEED PUDDING WITH BERRIES AND COCONUT MILK	BAKED TILAPIA WITH TOMATO AND OLIVE RELISH	MOROCCAN CHICKEN STEW	FRESH FRUIT SALAD
22	WHOLE GRAIN PANCAKES WITH BLUEBERRIES AND FLAXSEED	PAN-SEARED TILAPIA WITH TOMATOES AND OLIVES	KALE CHIPS WITH OLIVE OIL AND SEA SALT	GRILLED PEACHES WITH HONEY
24	EGG SCRAMBLE WITH BELL PEPPERS, TOMATOES, AND SPINACH	LENTIL AND SWEET POTATO CURRY	QUINOA CRACKERS WITH HUMMUS	LEMON BARS WITH ALMOND CRUST
25	OMELET WITH MUSHROOMS, ONIONS, AND FETA CHEESE	BLACK BEAN AND VEGETABLE ENCHILADAS	DEVILED EGGS WITH AVOCADO	MANGO LASSI
26	YOGURT BOWL WITH BERRIES, NUTS, AND SEEDS	WHITE BEAN AND KALE SOUP	BERRY SMOOTHIE WITH CHIA SEEDS	MIXED BERRY SORBET
27	SMOOTHIE BOWL WITH SPINACH, BANANA, AND CHIA SEEDS	MINESTRONE SOUP	Mixed Nuts With Dried Fruit	OAT AND FRUIT BARS
28	BREAKFAST BURRITO WITH SWEET POTATOES, BLACK BEANS, AND AVOCADO	LENTIL AND VEGETABLE SOUP	MOROCCAN CHICKEN STEW	PAPAYA BOATS WITH LIME AND MINT
29	AVOCADO TOAST WITH POACHED EGG AND SMOKED SALMON	MINESTRONE SOUP	SALMON AND VEGETABLE	QUINOA PUDDING WITH CINNAMON AND HONEY
30	BREAKFAST FRITTATA WITH VEGGIES AND FETA CHEESE	TURKEY AND WILD RICE SOUP	WHITE BEAN AND KALE SOUP	ROASTED PLUMS WITH VANILLA AND CINNAMON

Recipies Index

GRILLED BEEF WITH GARLIC AND ROSEMARY	59
GRILLED CHICKEN BREAST WITH HERBS AND LEMON	52
GRILLED EGGPLANT WITH BASIL AND MOZZARELLA	29
GRILLED EGGPLANT WITH TAHINI AND LEMON	72
GRILLED LAMB CHOPS WITH MINT AND LEMON	54
GRILLED LAMB WITH YOGURT AND CUCUMBER	57
GRILLED PEACHES WITH HONEY	79
GRILLED PORTOBELLO MUSHROOMS WITH BALSAMIC VINEGAR	33
GRILLED SALMON WITH LEMON AND HERBS	44
GRILLED SHRIMP SKEWERS WITH LEMON AND GARLIC	46
GRILLED SHRIMP WITH LIME AND CILANTRO	51
GRILLED SWORDFISH WITH MANGO SALSA	47
GRILLED ZUCCHINI WITH PARMESAN	30
GUACAMOLE WITH VEGGIES	72
KALE CHIPS WITH OLIVE OIL AND SEA SALT	73
LEMON BARS WITH ALMOND CRUST	79
LENTIL AND BUTTERNUT SQUASH CASSEROLE	38
LENTIL AND KALE SOUP	64
LENTIL AND SWEET POTATO CURRY	35
LENTIL DIP WITH VEGGIES	73
MANGO LASSI	79
MINESTRONE SOUP	67
MIXED BERRY SORBET	80
Mixed Nuts With Dried Fruit	74
MOROCCAN CHICKEN STEW	63
OAT AND FRUIT BARS	80
OAT AND SEED BARS WITH HONEY	74
OMELET WITH MUSHROOMS, ONIONS, AND FETA CHEESE	22
OVERNIGHT OATS WITH CHIA SEEDS, BERRIES, AND ALMOND MILK	19
PAN-FRIED SARDINES WITH LEMON AND OREGANO	48
PAN-SEARED BEEF WITH GARLIC AND MUSHROOM	53
PAN-SEARED PORK WITH GINGER AND SOY SAUCE	56
PAN-SEARED PORK WITH LEMON AND OREGANO	59
PAN-SEARED TILAPIA WITH TOMATOES AND OLIVES	50
PAN-SEARED TUNA WITH WASABI AIOLI	45
PAPAYA BOATS WITH LIME AND MINT	81
POACHED SALMON WITH DILL AND CUCUMBER	48
POACHED SALMON WITH LEMON AND PARSLEY	49
POPCORN WITH NUTRITIONAL YEAST AND SEA SALT	74
QUINOA AND BLACK BEAN STUFFED PEPPERS	40
QUINOA BOWL WITH VEGGIES, AVOCADO, AND A POACHED EGG	20

Kitchen Measurement Abbreviations (Standard and Metric)

Abbreviation	Measurement
tbsp	tablespoon
tsp	teaspoon
oz	ounce
fl. oz	fluid ounce
c	cup
qt	quart
pt	pint
gal	gallon
lb	pound
mL	milliliter
g	grams
kg	kilogram
l	liter

Dry Measurements Conversion Chart

Teaspoons	Tablespoons	Cups
3 tsp	1 tbsp	1/16 c
6 tsp	2 tbsp	1/8 c
12 tsp	4 tbsp	1/4 c
24 tsp	8 tbsp	1/2 c
36 tsp	12 tbsp	3/4 c
48 tsp	16 tbsp	1 c

Liquid Measurements Conversion Chart

Fluid Ounces	Cups	Pints	Quarts	Gallons
8 fl. oz	1 c	1/2 pt	1/4 qt	1/16 gal
16 fl. oz	2 c	1 pt	1/2 qt	1/8 gal
32 fl. oz	4 c	2 pt	1 qt	1/4 gal
64 fl. oz	8 c	4 pt	2 qt	1/2 gal
128 fl. oz	16 c	8 pt	4 qt	1 gal

Butter Measurements Chart

Sticks	Cups	Tablespoons	Ounces	Grams
1/2 stick	1/4 c	4 tbsp	2 oz	57.5 g
1 stick	1/2 c	8 tbsp	4 oz	115 g
2 sticks	1 c	16 tbsp	8 oz	230 g

Oven Temperatures Conversion

(Degrees) Celsius	(Degrees) Fahrenheit
120 C	250 F
160 C	320 F
180 C	350 F
205 C	400 F
220 C	425 F

Weight Equivalents US Standard Metric (approximate)

½ ounce	15 g
1 ounce	30 g
2 ounces	60 g
4 ounces	115 g
8 ounces	225 g
12 ounces	340 g

SCAN ME!

Printed in Great Britain
by Amazon

44928445R00051